PUTTING PAKISTAN RIGHT

*Standpoints on the War on Terror, Energy,
Transit Corridors & Economic Development*

by
MOAZZAM HUSAIN

ACKNOWLEDGEMENTS

The idea for this book originated over discussions with my class fellow Zehra Mahoon during our class reunion week in the summer of 2015 in Istanbul, Turkey. Zehra suggested for me to put together my various writings and ideas in a book so they could be more widely disseminated to reach a larger audience, which she felt they should. Without her guidance and tireless efforts at helping get it published, this book may not have been possible.

Most of the writings appeared as op-ed articles in Pakistan's Dawn newspaper between 2009 – 15. I must thank my editor, Ayesha Azfar of Dawn for meticulous content editing and fact checking. Also for her help with suggesting topics, developing ideas and generally encouraging me to write.

My brother Khurram Husain who's early encouragement led me to continue writing after I had written the first few pieces, my parents for the emotional support and scores of my readers who have engaged me on the ideas and opinions; and with many of whom I have developed lasting friendships.

Dedication

To my parents

INTRODUCTION

This is not an academic piece, neither a journalistic perspective on events. Instead the book contains perspectives gained from living and working in Pakistan and from talking to a cross section of Pakistani society. These perspectives open windows on some key themes which are addressed in this book: Pakistan's struggle against religious extremism, energy shortages, its position as a transit corridor and issues it faces in urban and economic development. These themes are often intertwined.

Each of these themes is further fleshed out and illustrated by short pieces that offer vistas into the fundamental issues that need to be overcome. Pakistan is a troubled country. On that there would be widespread consensus.

This easy to read and simple to understand template hopes to leave the reader with a deeper appreciation on the issues facing contemporary Pakistan and what needs to be done to put them right.

TABLE OF CONTENTS

OWNING
THE WAR ON TERROR

CAPTURE OF SARAROGHA FORT

Pakistan's has been a conventional military, trained for conventional warfare on its eastern front. Historically there has been nominal deployment on the Western border with Afghanistan. The Frontier Corps (FC), a lightly armed paramilitary force raised during the British colonial period has patrolled the frontier. Pakistan had not foreseen nor was prepared for the guerilla onslaught that was to come, in the years following 9/11.

January 2008

It is baffling how 400 Taliban fighters, indicating a battalion-sized force, had overrun and captured the Sararogha Fort. These forts, built by the British, were intended to serve as outposts. The purpose of such forward military bases is to observe insurgent activity, to patrol the area and to block the enemy from threatening the local population.

The Sararogha Fort sits on a ridge overlooking the Razmak-Jandola Road. Given that the insurgents were carrying heavy weaponry, mortars and rocket launchers, it is unlikely that they came on foot. To transport such a force with their munitions would require a convoy of minimum 40 vehicles.

The terrain is rugged – there are patches of pine forest, also some agricultural plots mostly terraced, but for the most part, are rocky. Mean elevation is 2,000m – peaks at 2,200m and valleys at 1,800m. In this time of rain, the area is well watered by torrential streams. As a result, the off-road terrain is 'unjeepable' Razmak to Sararogha segment.

As is usual in night operations, the convoy would have waited till sundown and then mobilised — indicating 5.30pm local time. The attack itself commenced at 9pm, which means they must have arrived at a safe nearby spot around 8pm and begun to regroup and take positions for the assault. This indicates a two-and-a-half hours travel time.

If the 40-odd vehicles travelled in a single convoy from start, then it could well have come out of the pine forested Shawal Mountains that straddle the Afghan border. These mountains can be seen from Razmak and are less than 50 miles from the Sararogha Fort. Alternatively, several smaller convoys of four to five vehicles, hidden in the small residential settlements, could have converged on the main road from different directions. This mode would generate considerable wireless chatter that savvy intelligence can pick up. In either mode, the convoys would be travelling with headlights off except for the lead vehicle — a suspicious thing even for a casual onlooker.

It is baffling that a convoy of 40 vehicles carrying armed Taliban, travelling on the main road for several miles can elude intelligence, roadside checkposts and aerial surveillance.

The operation commenced around 9pm with the Taliban breaching a hole in the wall of the fort using explosives. Even then, the 38 FC personnel held off the invading battalion for six hours. When did the FC HQ receive the first distress signal? Was it communicated to their commander?

Did the commander request for reinforcements for his men in trouble? What is the standard operating procedure in an event of this nature?

As the FC men fought on, was a request sent to the Army Aviation squadrons under the Peshawar Corps to send in the Cobra AH1-F attack helicopters — eight of which are night-capable (C-NITE equipped)? Did the Ludda Fort nearby receive a distress call requesting artillery fire on the Taliban position? What artillery equipment was available to it and who was going to make the decision? Was it in artillery range and were the Taliban's coordinates known?

Apart from rescuing the lives of the 38 FC personnel and the morale of all other FC personnel, this was an opportunity to take out 400 Taliban fighters – thereby striking a major blow to their operations in the area.

The Taliban butchered and captured the FC personnel, and after removing ammunition and communications equipment, set the fort on fire and made their way back probably reaching their safe havens before sunrise. Again, nobody saw where the 40 vehicles carrying armed Taliban went, and so they live to fight another day.

This brings us to the question: Are we conducting our national fight against these elements to the best of our abilities? This is the real battle for Pakistan. I would urge Gen Kayani to hold an inquest into this case. I am concerned that in the not too distant future we may be facing a Taliban assault force of brigade strength.

PEACE DEALS AND OTHER BLUNDERS

From the colonial period, Pakistan's tribal areas have been lightly governed, allowing local custom and tradition to take precedence. One of the principles is for tribes to take responsibility for law and order in their respective jurisdictions. Another is for 'collective punishment' in the event of a breach. A system of tribal elders, known as 'jirga', which coordinates with local political authorities, had worked well for over a century. That system began to come undone after the US bombing campaign in Afghanistan following the events of September 11, 2001.

April 2009

TWO months into Operation Enduring Freedom, the fugitives` escape into Pakistan`s tribal areas was a foregone conclusion. That was the time to closely watch the Durand Line, not just the Khyber and Kurram agencies.

Even meagre efforts like mobile scout parties, tribal lashkars and airborne patrols would have sent a signal that Fata was not an open sanctuary. These efforts may have discouraged or even intercepted some of these 3,500 mule-trotting, heavily armed foreign fighters. They would have kept the trail hot for those that did manage to breach the Durand Line in the last few weeks of 2001.

As was expected, fleeing Al Qaeda and other militants notably those from the Islamic Movement of Uzbekistan, members of the Chechen resistance movement, Chinese Uighur fighters and other smaller groups rode into Pakistan and set up camp around Angoor Adda in South Waziristan.

We can all beat up on Tommy Franks later for taking his eye off the ball but that doesn`t absolve us from taking ours off the Durand Line. That was our first blunder.

Now with these foreign fighters inside its borders, what did Pakistan do in response? The short answer is `nothing`. The long answer is that right until the spring of 2004 Pakistan did nothing to prevent foreign fugitives from settling in areas under its control. It did nothing to prevent them from forming local linkages often beyond the tribal areas. It did nothing to stop them from carrying out subsequent attacks across the Durand Line.

In this window of time, space and resources, Al Qaeda scaled up its 055 Brigade into a full-fledged shadow army. The Lashkar-i-Zil, as it is called, has come to permeate the Taliban and all other foreign and local jihadi groups. In the recent Swat footage its soldiers are discernable — heads covered in hoods, generally better dressed, wearing green military jackets with stashes of AK- 47 magazines, shalwars above ankles and sneakers.

Blunder number two came when we lost the opportunity to mop up the local jihadi outfits lock, stock and barrel. The writing was on the wall in black and bold Pakistani jihadis were redundant liabilities with no place in the new world at least in the foreseeable future. A swift dragnet operation could have put them out of business in one single stroke.

Instead we got the famous U-turn speech of January 2002 and a light-fisted crackdown that only drove these outfits underground and eventually out of the intelligence orbit altogether. They subsequently resurfaced in the tribal areas.

The third blunder was Kalosha, a badly planned military operation, with disastrous consequences. Fast forward to March 2004. Location Azam Warsak where Tahir Yuladashev was holed up with 300 fighters of the Islamic Movement of Uzbekistan, an Al Qaeda affiliate. An intelligence estimate of their position and strength existed with the ISI but was not shared with the FC and the army. On being surrounded, the IMU fighters fought ferociously and then tore through the cordon riding Toyota pick-ups with mounted missile launchers.

Inflicting 200 casualties on the FC, the Al Qaeda fighters broke away to link up with reinforcements — the forces of Pakistani Taliban commander Nek Mohammad. Soon helicopter gunships were called in. However the can of worms had been opened and the fighting spread all over Wana. South Waziristan was now on fire.

What could have been a short, precise and hard-hitting operational plan in a localised area no more than 40 square miles turned out to be a bungle with disastrous implications.

When did our war courses stop teaching how to employ stealth, surprise and deception in combat operations? What happened to our Special Forces? Why aren`t field and electronic intelligence and psychological operations being utilised to inflict maximum and targeted damage on the enemy? Have we considered engaging the enemy in surprise locations with night operations deploying the advantage of night vision equipment, and the eight Cobra attack helicopters that are C-Nite equipped? How often have these capabilities been used and to what effect?

Nek Mohammad was subsequently taken out in a US drone attack.

Over time 80,000 additional troops were sent into South Waziristan. The rebels responded in classic guerrilla style — by enlarging the battle theatre to include North Waziristan and subsequently Mohmand and Bajaur. The capture and burning of the Sararogha Fort was particularly indicative of the enemy`s ability to organise and undertake operations in battalion-sized formations. This was an important milestone indicating that a guerrilla movement, in a matter of six bungled years, had come of age.

More recently in Bajaur, the Taliban have demonstrated the capability to beat back a frontal assault. In Al Jazeera`s documentary `Pakistan`s War on the Frontline`, tanks and infantry of the 63rd FF regiment are seen retreating in panic after encountering Taliban fire. The reporter Rageh Omar describes the Pakistani tank commander as "quite shaken". Ominously, the footage shows Lashkar-i-Zil`s sophisticated work — trench and tunnel networks and bunkers that are largely beyond the reach of the Pakistani military`s limited `hard target` capability.

According to Pakistani writer Ahmed Rashid, it was military blunders that convinced the Americans in 2006 to intervene with more drone and missile attacks to assist a beleaguered military that was now largely hunkered in its bases and cantonments (with the exception of Bajaur). With its men losing morale and its (as well as Nato`s) hardware being captured or destroyed by the Taliban, the fourth blunder was to enter into a series of `peace deals` with groups of highly organised and armed Islamist rebels.American commentator Bill Roggio learnt of the terms of the truce from an anonymous US intelligence source. Writing in the Long War Journal in 2006, he likens it to an instrument of surrender the military was to evacuate Waziristan after handing over all seized weapons and equipment. An unknown quantity of money was also transferred to the Taliban.

Some 130 Al Qaeda members were released from Pakistani prisons and allowed to remain in what the truce referred to as the Islamic Emirate of Waziristan for the governance of which, the document mentions, the Taliban and Al Qaeda have set up a `Mujahideen Shura`. Pakistani officials arriving at the soccer field for the signing were frisked for weapons by armed Taliban as Al Qaeda`s black flag, the Al Rayah, hung over the scoreboard of the stadium.

Referring to the Swat deal Hasan Askari Rizvi, professor of political science, terms it as "co-opting the Taliban as an acceptable alternative to state governance or at best making them partners with the state, instead of subjects of the state".So the question once again is could we have played the hand we were dealt any better? I will leave this for the reader to judge.

DEFINING THE WAR ON TERROR

In December 2007, Benazir Bhutto was assassinated. Weeks later her party, the Pakistan People's Party was voted to power. Until then, Pakistan had been losing the war to extremists.

February 2008

From the White House perspective, there is good news and bad news from Pakistan: The good news is that elections were held and by and large perceived to be free and fair. Bad news: The Musharaf backed alliance was routed. Good news: The forces that won are more moderate and secular than their predecessors. Bad news: As the Taliban regroup for their spring offensive, there is a prevailing sense of uncertainty in Washington as to the nature of Pakistan's future role in the war on terror.

The good news is that the winners in the elections are already talking about giving a Pakistani definition to this war. In Pakistan, this translates to an approach that can pointedly lower the profile, scale and intensity of the conflict. Primarily, to fight an invisible enemy you need to couple invisible surveillance with an invisible force – a force that provides a rapid, agile and flexible response for execution of precise combat operations.

As part of its modernizing outlook, the Pakistan Army would do well to consider consolidating all aspects of war fighting under a Regional Unified Combatant Command for the Federally Administered Tribal Areas. (RUCC-FATA). This command would have under it detachments of regular army troops, all paramilitary forces in the region, a special forces battalion, attack and transport helicopters, ground attack aircraft, field and electronic intelligence, psychological operations, the whole nine yards.

With these resources, RUCC-FATA would be tasked to a) keep all main and secondary roads safe and well policed, b) protect the local population against threats/intimidation from the Taliban, c) protect utility, communications, education and government nfrastructure/installations and d) restrict and regulate cross border movement across the Durand line, the de facto frontier between Pakistan and Afghanistan. In this way the military campaign can be conducted effectively freeing up the rest of the army to carry on in business as usual mode.

The second part, invisible surveillance, results from documentation and analysis of data from movement – principally of vehicles, telecoms traffic and people. Curfews, blockades and suspension of telecom services have the opposite effect. They choke the creation of data. It is also inordinately difficult to infiltrate intelligence moles into cordoned off areas where populations are bottled in.

Needless to say US forces participating in operations in Pakistani territory is a sensitive subject in Pakistan. However, with unmanned aerial vehicles operating from Pakistani airfields and bearing Pakistani markings, the distinction can be blurred.

Turning to surveillance, a system of chip based smart ID cards primarily intended to differentiate combatants from non combatants and to ease movement would be the cornerstone of an enrolment and registration system. A luring value proposition is to offer it as an entry ticket into a system of privilege, linking people with each other and offering subsidized food and micro-credit.

A similar initiative to fit all vehicles moving inside, or entering and leaving the tribal areas with a tamper proof GPS tracking device would need heavy subsidy, but is viable particularly if it is enforced through regular and irregular checks and tied in with a fuel subsidy. Military vehicles need to be equipped for a different reason. In a recent incident it took the army some days to recover its ammunition laden trucks that had been seized by the Taliban. Finally a subsidized CDMA "telephone for every household" scheme would link the registered population with each other as well as to an emergency response line.

USAID and other American planners are grappling with the question of the present system's capacity to deliver the promised US $ 750m in aid for FATA with the additional worry that the money doesn't fall into the wrong hands. These initiatives address both their concerns. The resulting free movement and free flow of aid would offer the local people an enabling environment in which they have both a stake, and a viable alternative to Talibanism.

Despite Benazir Bhutto's assassination, secular forces have come to fore in these elections. This has undoubtedly thrown a spanner into Al Qaeda's operational strategy that aimed to crumble the state and society in

Pakistan. However, its leadership and infrastructure not only remains intact but has established a network of sleeper cells in Pakistani cities. In all probability, Al Qaeda's new strategy would be one of self preservation, under which these cells would remain dormant. They would only be activated as a means of imposing a cost on the Pakistani state if it threatens Al Qaeda's existence, or its ability to conduct worldwide terror strikes.

This is a catch 22 situation for the new government for which Washington would be well advised to consider underwriting the premium and insurance cover if Al Qaeda is to be denied the time, space and strength it seeks to create. This is a long war and it's far from over.

WHAT OBAMA WILL NOT HEAR FROM ZARDARI?

Shortly afterwards, Pakistan launched a series of aggressive military operations to retake areas under Taliban control. The US supported the actions with military assistance while at the same time implored Pakistan to "do more". The "do more" alluded to acting against the safe havens primarily in North Wazirstan where the Haqqani group, a Taliban affiliate and other foreign fighters were lodged. Against this backdrop, President Zardari prepared to undertake a visit to Washington. But there were a few things the Americans needed to appreciate.

May 2009

NOW that the tide of Pakistani public opinion appears to be turning against the Taliban and as the military scores a series of successes, Pakistan needs to be given an enabling environment to follow this process through to its logical conclusion.

The Obama administration and congressional policymakers may not hear this from President Zardari and the Pakistani delegation when they arrive in Washington this week. But policymakers in Washington would do well to approach policy formulation from the perspective of Pakistan's overall military doctrine as it has evolved after 1971.

The defeat and dismemberment of Pakistan in 1971 had left deep scars on both the military and society. The "1000-year war" with India that then President Z.A. Bhutto spoke of was a populist response as much as an early conception of a defensive people's guerilla war against future Indian interventionism.

While on a visit to China, Bhutto had shared his dilemma with then Chinese premier Zhou En-Lai:

Bhutto: How does one reconcile a poor country and a strong army?

Zhou: "Build a people's army, like we did in China."

A subsequent communique to Tikka Khan, his commander-in-chief, perhaps best summarised Bhutto's thinking in which he wrote:

"There will no longer be an absence of clear thinking from our side. In the remotest of our villages, the humblest of our people possess a self-confidence, a

ready willingness to march forward into India — a spirit, the equivalent of which cannot be found on the other side."

Even though at the time the army laughed off the proposition, the bug made its way into its doctrinal thinking — even as Pakistani officers at the Staff College in Quetta were being taught that only states with a strong ideological orientation and tight social solidarity like China and North Vietnam can have an effective people's army. In the background, this strain was beginning to fuse with the tradition of American training of Pakistani Special Forces.

The synthesis when combined with the 1000-year tradition of tribal guerilla warfare that exists in the NWFP and Balochistan resulted in a new variant of the people's war doctrine that said "train and arm friendly populations in the territory of your enemy, tying him down in a hundred places".

This doctrine was tested successfully against the Soviets in the 1980s and in Kashmir in the 1990s until it ran into problems due to two factors: Its unacceptability post 9/11 and the induction of nuclear-capable, short-range tactical surface-to-surface missiles into the arsenals of India and Pakistan.

It is inevitable that the Pakistan Army, if not already, will soon begin to rethink and reformulate this doctrine. Changes to the military's C3I (command, control, communications and intelligence) structure will not be far behind. In its logical extension it will also include large-scale screening of all officers and ranks for ideological orientation as well as military counter intelligence to watch for any sympathisers of Islamist rebels — as these elements can have a devastating effect on motivation, morale and discipline within the ranks.

In doing so, a relaxation in three binding constraints would significantly enlarge Pakistan's menu of strategic choices. The constraints I'm referring to are the question of the Durand Line, the alleged interference in Balochistan, and, most importantly, the question of the disputed territory of Kashmir.

The US with unifying support from the international community needs to help Pakistan and its neighbours resolve these, thereby giving Pakistan a large canvas on which to draw its new military doctrine. Without creating that room, no matter how many times you simulate this in game theory — a state with a weak economy, with unresolved boundaries and disputed territories — each time the Pakistani hawks will prevail. This will be by proving themselves right with cost-effective doctrines like "our people's ready willingness to march into India" or the more successful "train and arm friendly populations in the territory of your enemy, tying him down in a hundred places".

In a country where the military doctrine is central, Gen Petraeus for instance, would do well to spend a day with Pakistani generals and assess the following scenario: An Afghan National Army has been raised. Nato has pulled out except for a nominal presence in Kabul where an Afghan government hostile to Pakistan has come to power. With Gen Petraeus in the shoes of a Pakistani general, how does the situation look? Where are the separatist Baloch likely to be located? And which side of the line are the opponents to the new Afghan government to be found? As a commander, what are the military options? How does the scenario pan out from here?

Armed with such insights, Gen Petraeus would find himself better equipped to explain the realities to the Senate's armed services committee. The reality of life in a rough, lawless neighbourhood. The reality of one neighbour laying claim to half your property and refusing to put a fence in between, another neighbour occupying what you think is half of your vegetable garden and then stealing water from your hosepipe by cutting a leak in it even while you're looking. The reality of a long list of grievances of having been, at different times, wronged, robbed, roughed up, broken up and, as Hillary Clinton recently admitted, abandoned.

The key to peace in this region may lie with the Obama administration facilitating a negotiated settlement of the Durand Line as the final border between the two countries, by perhaps re-tasking Richard Boucher to put Kashmir high up on the international agenda of unresolved international disputes awaiting final settlement and by assisting in bringing the insurgency in Balochistan to an end.

Billions of dollars of aid money given to Egypt, to Pakistan, to Jordan, even to Palestine may have brought about temporary behavioural compliance. But the greenbacks alone did not change the way in which the public perceives the US in these countries. So in terms an additional payoff, a US that is seen to be helping end territorial disputes, settling borders and extinguishing fires will cast itself in a different light.

The halo will be seen from far and the ripples felt on the streets and ghettos of major cities in the Islamic world and across the Muslim diasporas beyond. This is a blank cheque the US will in effect be writing to itself.

DO WE KNOW THE ENEMY?

As military successes continued, Pakistanis were appalled to learn that Pakistan was fighting a creed of religiously inspired violent extremists who sought to impose a religious order based on Shariah using violent means. Many were in denial; others spun conspiracy theories to escape the uncomfortable truth. Meanwhile the right wing political parties cried out for negotiations with their extremist co-religionists. This was to remain a major impediment to the state's resolve to prosecute this war.

May 2009

WAITING in line to drive through an army checkpoint on the leafy Shami Road of Lahore garrison, my driver hesitatingly utters "Sir, can I ask you a question?" "Yes sure," I tell him. "This is all a game isn't it.... Ultimately they want to take away our nuclear weapons ... don't they sir?"

With military operations under way in Dir, Buner and Swat and the question coming from a retired infantry soldier who is now employed as my driver I assume the "they" means the Taliban, the troublemakers, the Islamists, the militants, the rebels or some such. Still, to be sure I ask who wants to take them away. "Why, the Americans, the Jews, the Indians of course. After all they are the ones funding the Taliban!" he exclaims.

I stare out of the windscreen and let my mind wander ... to Islamabad, Constitution Avenue, to the information ministry. Do the folks there know how ordinary Pakistanis are thinking? Does this ministry even have a mission statement? NGOs and citizen's groups — with meagre resources — have launched campaigns and held protest marches. We have even heard isolated utterances from members of the clergy, on how the Quran forbids suicide bombings. Even Al Qaeda and the Tehrik-i-Taliban have media cells to give a populist spin to their ideology so that it finds maximum resonance.

On the other hand, there is no visible attempt from Pakistan's Ministry of Information to develop a systematic campaign as a counter narrative to this toxicity. If not the information ministry where in the haystack of our ministries and government departments will I find this needle? A narrative that will also get the respective constituencies of

Nawaz Sharif, Imran Khan and the religious parties to ask if you want to negotiate with the Taliban then first decide, is the constitution of Pakistan negotiable? Is our democracy negotiable? Is the Supreme Court of Pakistan negotiable? Is the state's writ negotiable? Are the custodial controls of our nuclear weapons negotiable? The first rule of negotiation is that you do not come to the table empty-handed. The second rule is that you have to be prepared to give away something.

As the car comes to a stop at the barrier I realise I am looking directly at a beard, and then up at the face from which it originates — running halfway down the chest. There is no turban, instead a red beret and the military police armband. In place of an AK-47 and rocket launcher slung over the shoulder, the weapon is an MP 5, held — as a professional soldier would hold it — slung down to the hip, one hand on the weapon.

Witnessing a Pakistan Army exercise some years ago, Colonel Brian Cloughley, who was then Australian defence attache in Islamabad, had crawled into a dug-in artillery observation post. Inside a young officer had shown him a laser range finder — a device used to measure distance. As Cloughley was examining the high-tech device, the officer treated him to an exposition of how there is in fact no need for advanced technology, if one believes in Allah.

On another occasion he was informed by a junior officer on how the beard of one of his soldiers had turned red on its own ... in fact because of the piety displayed during his recent Haj. The commanding officer had buried his head in his hands but had made no comment.

For the most part, personnel deployed at nuclear sites are screened. As a matter of principle, why not extend this precaution to cover all members of the military? In this way, the primary role of military counter-intelligence would be to watch for any sympathisers.

As a means to guarding the rear, a systematic programme to curtail the undesirable activities of the clergy would be immensely effective. In the first instance they should be persuaded to change sides. Preaching in mosques needs to be put under the control of the security apparatus of the state. Mosques and clergy under strong state control can be made to function as a powerful via media through which to disseminate the counter jihadi narrative.

With the space closing in on Al Qaeda as a result of the above initiatives its response will be to turn down the volume of the conflict in Swat (and Fata) to a low-intensity war of attrition. After it has drawn the army into the valleys and the Taliban have fled, Al Qaeda's 055 Brigade and diehard Taliban will dig in. They will seek to bog down the army through suicide bombings at checkpoints, hit its convoys with roadside improvised explosive devices, and carry out guerrilla hit-and-run operations on its supply lines.

During this drawn-out conflict, Al Qaeda will seek to precipitate another crisis with India. It is therefore important that this time the army should eliminate and net as many militants as operationally possible. This is best done by blocking their exit routes out of Swat and follow up by combing the area in a dragnet operation.

Back at the checkpoint, the Suzuki Bolan van ahead of us is waved through. Driving it is a burly bearded fellow wearing a skullcap. A kid occupies the front seat, also wearing a skullcap and two veiled black bodies are on the back seat. Seen from the corner of the eye an unremarkable Toyota Corolla except for a US college sticker on its rear windshield has been pulled over. The occupants, two young boys, one wearing studded jeans another in knee-length shorts, stand facing a security man. He is casually checking their documents but appears more amused by one's tattooed arm and the other's pierced eyebrow. Another one snickers as he casually checks the car.

As we pass through, my mind is once again wandering — would the driver of that van, the man in the skullcap; condone the negotiating away of our constitution? What about that officer that, Col Brian Cloughley had met at the war exercise — the one who thought you didn't need sophisticated technology if you believed in Allah. What if he's guarding our nuclear weapons right now? It wanders still further ... to President Zardari using the metaphor of cancer to describe the Talibanisation of Pakistan. Isn't that when healthy cells turn malignant and rapidly multiply? And I thought we said we knew what the enemy looks like.

FIGHT TO THE FINISH

Finally, using ground and airborne troops, Special Forces and night strike aircraft, Pakistan conducted Operation Rah-e-Raast, which, till that point was its longest battle in history. The unsurprising result was a decisive victory for Pakistan's armed forces. The districts of Swat, Buner, Dir and Shangla were cleared of approximately 5,000 Taliban militants. Their commander Mullah Fazlullah escaped to Afghanistan.

June 2009

A SKILLED female worker in a garment factory in Bangladesh or Sri Lanka generates $2 in value added per hour. In terms of the $2-per-day poverty line this pulls a family of six out of poverty. A call centre attendant in Mumbai or Bangalore generates $5 per hour and a computer programmer could do upwards of $20 per hour or $40,000 GDP per capita.

If finance adviser Shaukat Tarin were to do a back-of-the-envelope calculation, he may find, arguably, that each gun-toting militant in Pakistan perhaps destroys economic value equivalent to 25 times this — to the tune of $1m. This is the cost each militant imposes on the economy each year. We will turn to the numbers in a moment.

According to early reports on the electronic media, the cost of Operation Rah-i-Raast in the first few days had blown a hole in excess of Rs50bn in the exchequer. By the time the operation is over, the cost could well have touched $1.5bn. Every dollar here will be incremental to the defence budget.

Add to that, the cost of relief efforts for the IDPs which adviser Tarin himself estimates at $800m and the forgone earnings of the three million people of Swat from agriculture, tourism, mining, trade and transport. That will be another $750m taken at Pakistan's per capita average of $1,000 for three months' losses. You see where we are getting at? Yes we're getting to $3bn and we're also getting to next week's budget speech. Sitting deep in an impregnable base in the Hindu Kush mountains, Al Qaeda will be listening to this speech with a lot of interest.

In addition to tough fiscal measures, expect to see government borrowing rise and inflation and interest rates creep up again. With little fiscal room, the government will resort to borrowing and printing money to finance Rah-i-Raast. Time is on the opposite side here and Al Qaeda's planned strategy would quite predictably be to switch to a low-intensity war of attrition mode, keep the army in Swat, keep the IDPs out and bleed the exchequer till the State Bank says "ouch". To frustrate this strategy, it is important to deny Al Qaeda any operational sanctuaries in Swat. The hand of effective governance must also move into Swat as IDPs return.

Back to the numbers; $3bn to rid Swat of 3,000 hard-core militants. At the rate of $1m each, every long-haired, bearded gun-toting militant has negated one year of work of 25 software programmers or of a small software house or of a 100-seat call centre. Alternately each Taliban has destroyed the economic value created by 250 garment workers, a rather not-so-small garment factory, in addition to driving away business for many others. And that is counting tangible losses only. We have not factored in the image loss to Pakistan that my friends in advertising refer to as "negative brand equity".

We have not counted the sufferings of the genuine visa-seekers, and the distress caused to the overseas diaspora of patriotic Pakistanis, the cost of export orders lost and better prices our products could have commanded in international trade and the loss of investment that Pakistan had to suffer.

Add to this the cost of scaring away potentially lucrative business joint venture relationships, the cost of scaring away airlines, tourism, cricket teams. The loss of not seeing the delightful sight of thousands of foreigners coming to Pakistan each year on exchange visits, as students, volunteer workers in NGOs and charities, on internships and for adventure tourism. The loss of similar opportunities that would have been accorded to the youth of Pakistan to go on reciprocal exchange visits. The numbing down of the feeling that Pakistan is part of a bigger world and that Pakistanis are global citizens.

I had written earlier that "the post Taliban era must soon begin". This was intended in a rhetorical sense only. We need to in fact prepare for a long war. My sense is that given a few right tools the Pakistani military may be able to get the job done faster and at a lower cost. It can get it done at fewer risks to itself and with lower collateral damage.

One of these tools is the JDAM (joint direct attack munitions). Basically this is a GPS guidance kit that can retrofit onto a 1000-2000 lb conventional bomb. Using the F-16s' advanced avionics, continuously updated GPS data steers the bomb to target accuracy within 6-8 metres. At a cost of $14,000 it turns a dumb bomb into a 'near smart' munitions with target homing capability approximating a high-precision laser-guided weapon. The JDAM has been successfully battle-tested. During the peak of Operation Enduring Freedom in Afghanistan, 3,000 of these were being used each month by the US air force and navy.

I had earlier suggested the need for the information ministry to develop a counter-narrative to Al Qaeda's ideology of global jihad to disabuse the notion that we are fighting 'America's war'. Three war-fighting weeks later there are no signs of effort from this white elephant ministry; so before the Pakistan Air Force begins mounting the JDAMs on the pylons of its F-16s, and as Al Qaeda prepares to listen to the budget speech, I would like to use the opportunity accorded here. Our message is this:

'We are the children of the Indus basin, one of the world's largest natural resource and a cradle of ancient civilisations like Moenjodaro, Harappa and Gandhara that go back thousands of years. Today we are a multiethnic society sharing a rich history. Indeed our national language Urdu is an amalgam of Persian, Turkish, Arab, Central Asian and North Indian influences.

'Pakistan is our land, our home, rich in agriculture and mineral resources and alive with the spirit of enterprise of our hardworking people. Every inch of it is sacred and we treat it with reverence; and so we expect others who come here would behave, as one is supposed to behave when in someone else's home. You have come in here uninvited, of your own volition and have not treated our soil with the respect it is worthy of. Do not mistake our smiling faces, our large-heartedness and our simple manners for fickle-mindedness.

'Our God is benevolent, not angry and vindictive. Whilst proud of our homeland we are also citizens of a larger world that offers us opportunities to realise our larger aspirations. We can understand that the presence of American forces in Saudi Arabia during Operation Desert Storm in 1991 may have stoked your feelings, but today, your declaring jihad against your enemies, sitting on our soil outrages us.

'We are a nuclear-weapons state; we are proud of our military and our courageous people. We have friends around the world. We can look after our interests. We do not need you to fight for our causes. If you must fight for yours, then please go elsewhere. Take your foreign fighters and please leave. We ask you to leave and go find a home somewhere else.'

SPEAKING THE TRUTH

In many ways, the Pakistani military had itself been obfuscating the facts from its own people. Had this not been done, the consensus against fighting extremism would have evolved much sooner. Perhaps the officer corps felt this would help maintain better cohesion within the ranks, who may otherwise be enticed by the right wing narrative.

June 2009

THE view was panoramic from atop Peochar from where the operational commander of the Special Forces contingent informed a private TV channel that "the militants' leadership had fled by the time we got here".

He moved on to speculate on the sources of arms and funds for the Swat Taliban alluding to a "foreign hand". Within hours, rightwing blogs and discussion groups on the Internet were ablaze with activity. "See we told you, it was the Indians". We finally have "proof". Stop the operation ... stop fighting America's war, the noises came.

I tread with caution here before jumping to any conclusions. The guns are of Russian, American and Indian origin we are told. This is one data point. The source of funds is a question mark and thereby potentially another data point. Now let's consider a few more and then see if we can join the dots.

There is an international arms bazaar and some enterprising regional arms dealers. A variety of weapons are available in this region at a price. Moreover, the US ticket out of Afghanistan is a well-equipped, disciplined Afghan National Army (ANA) — becoming an effective counter-insurgency force before 2020. For now, the force has a high rate of dropout and desertion. Its arms inventory has Soviet bloc weapons. New recruits, when issued American arms, often choose to sell them after dropping out. Some soldiers desert to the Taliban who offer $300 per month as against $70 in the ANA.

Consider also that the cache of weapons recovered from Lal Masjid was stolen from inside the Aabpara police station in the heart of our capital. It's not just weapons that Nato loses in Afghanistan, sometimes its prisoners escape too. One of these was Abu Yahya al Libbi who on the night of July 10, 2005 along with three others escaped from the interim detention facility at the Bagram airbase. Libbi was one of the hundreds captured and interrogated by the Pakistani security establishment before being handed over to the Americans.

Al Qaeda today is a multinational organisation. It often does business under different brand names. Based on interrogation of suspects, the Egyptian interior ministry believes that the Feb 22 bombing in Khan el Khalili in Cairo was the work of an Al Qaeda cell masquerading as the Palestinian Islamic Army. The cell arranged paramilitary training in Gaza sending recruits there via tunnels under the border.

According to Al Ahram, Egypt's leading independent daily, the arrested suspects in the Khan el Khalili bombing include a French woman of Albanian origin, a British national of Egyptian descent, two Palestinians, a Belgian national of Tunisian descent and two Egyptians — multinational par excellence.

Al Qaeda's methods are modern. The organisation today operates in "network mode" indicating a cellular structure as opposed to a hierarchy. It can keep a low profile and its cells can build the capability of its affiliates by infusing the use of information technology and other tools of globalisation. So while the Tehrik-i-Taliban Pakistan destroys TVs, CDs and computers, Al Qaeda uses its video production facilities, websites and electronic bulletin boards as a force multiplier.

After escaping from Bagram, Libbi arrived in Swat and linked up with the Tehrik-i-Nifaz-i-Shariat Mohammadi (TNSM). With help from Libbi, Maulana Fazlullah's first illegal FM channel went on air in 2006. In time this pilot was scaled up into a successful propaganda machine with a series of elusive FM broadcast stations. These operated through portable transmission boxes of Chinese origin that could be mounted on trucks and even motorcycles. Libbi provided content development guidelines to Fazlullah: "Pakistan's army should be treated as an occupying infidel army waging an offensive war on an invaded Muslim population."

In the aftermath of the fall of the Lal Masjid in 2007, Al Qaeda arranged reinforcements for Swat from Baitullah Mehsud, its virtual proxy in Pakistan and host to a large contingent of foreign fighters. Uzbeks, Arabs and Chechens were sent to join Fazlullah's forces in Swat. Training camps were set up and a large recruitment drive initiated. Within two years Al Qaeda transformed a primitive organisation into a formidable political and military force. This force not only extracted an unprecedented and unanimous concession for implementation of Sharia from Pakistan's parliament but was later able to engage the Pakistani military in the longest battle of its history.

In terms of understanding the sources of funds for the Taliban, let's pick up another data point Tariq Azizuddin, the Pakistani ambassador to Afghanistan, was released after being held for three months by his Taliban kidnappers. According to Dawn newspaper, the Pakistan government released an unspecified number of militants and paid $2.5m in ransom. Kidnapping for ransom is the Taliban's second largest source of funds after narcotics. The released were associates of Taliban commander Mansoor Dadullah. It is very easy to ascertain who Dadullah works for. Pick up the ISI's tactical interrogation reports on the released associates. Had they indicated a foreign intelligence connection during interrogation? Indeed, had Abu Yahya al Libbi indicated any such connections?

Only such brutal honesty can lead the people of Pakistan to the exit door out of the present quagmire. By pointing the finger at others we may drop the ball again. At 2 pm on Oct 1, 2001, a jeep laden with explosives rammed into the Jammu and Kashmir legislative assembly in Srinagar. Jaish-i-Mohammad claimed responsibility for the attack. That same evening an as-yet-unexplained fire gutted the sensitive records portion of Pakistan Army's General Headquarters.

A month after the attack on the Indian parliament, President Musharraf made his famous "U-turn" speech in January 2002. Three days later another fire gutted the records, this time of the interior ministry on the 16th floor of the Shaheed-i-Millat secretariat in Islamabad's Blue Area. A dark chapter of Pakistani history may have been obliterated by these fires. But burning evidence of your past sins does not get you to a viable future.

The choices we make today will determine whether the 15-year-old in the madressah will — in 10 years time — emerge as a reformed, skilled and economically productive citizen of what will then be a modern state. Or whether he would have risen to become a warlord and will be seen negotiating with a foreign mining contractor for the grant of a concession to a full block of Thar coal — in what will possibly be a denuclearised Pakistan with a nominal government. By choosing to speak the truth today, we choose a better future.

COURAGE TO QUESTION

If the right wing narrative underpins extremist ideology, then a religio- nationalist obscurantism is the bedrock that lies beneath this right wing dogma. This is not the same thing as being illiterate. One could be educated yet inhabit a realm of intellectual darkness.

July 2009

IT'S sometimes tempting to think of the power crisis as a simplified model of the national crisis today. A large part of the role behind Japan's success was played by its corporations. Companies like Mitsubishi, Nissan and Sumitomo excelled by teaching their managers to ask questions.

For example, they would ask why we didn't meet our sales target last month. To the answer our production was slow, the follow-up question would be why it was slow. We're short of spare parts; machines kept breaking down, would come the answer. Why were we short of .... And in this way Japan probed its way to the bottom of its problems and very soon became a rich country.

Getting rich by asking questions? Why, sounds absurd? Not to the US Navy which then sported an "if it ain't broke, don't fix it" attitude. In 1984 it adopted the technique and — after adding additional content — branded it Total Quality Management. TQM became a buzzword and spread like wildfire to just about every US Corporation and onwards to Europe and Asia.

A few days ago, as the lights and air-conditioning suddenly died on me and I put down Dr (Justice) Javid Iqbal's book, Islam and Pakistan's Identity, the last words to stick in my mind were "Pakistan is not a failed state; it is in the hands of a 'failed generation'." Iqbal envisioned a homeland for Muslims, Maudoodi, counter-intuitively, resisted on two counts: One, a separate Muslim state would limit Islam which had not fully done its work in India. Two, that the Musalmans of India were not 'pure' enough (read not fundamentalist enough) to be deserving of an all-Muslim state. Iqbal retorted that "Muslim state and society were always in a process of becoming and never became a finished product."

Nevertheless there were problems with Iqbal's approach, as he too maintained that the religious ideal could not be separated from the social order. Was he implying an Islamic state (or republic)? Because once you're on that turf aren't you left with little room for debate about implementing Sharia? Isn't it setting you up as a target for a fundamentalist onslaught that an unfulfilled promise of an 'Islamic Republic' brings on?

Unlike his predecessors Ziaul Haq not only gave way to this onslaught, he harnessed it. Then again in the summer of 1998 came another close call. That year, with his intended 15th Amendment, Nawaz Sharif brought Pakistan within inches of becoming a theocratic state. By 1998 weren't Iqbal, Maudoodi, Zia and Nawaz Sharif all on the same page? True, Jinnah hadn't wanted an Islamic state; just a state for Muslims but then, doesn't the basis for Pakistan boil down to Muslims being only able to live with other Muslims?

The lights flickered back on, the AC started to hiss and the reassuring hum of appliances could be heard again. Then they dimmed and finally died again. Is there a power shortage? Apparently not. By some accounts, installed capacity is enough to meet all except peak demand. So why the blackouts? Circular debt ... Mangla tripped ... Lesco's transformer at the Kot Lakhpat grid gave way. In the end we may find that there was less a shortage of capacity, and more a shortage of intelligent questions; and an inability to clear a cobweb of stupidity.

So if Dr (Justice) Javid Iqbal's lament is that Pakistan is in the hands of a failed generation Aitzaz Ahsan, in his book, The Indus Saga, explains why. "Pakistanis have spent almost half a century of their existence without asking any questions." Indeed bold, courageous and informed questions are anathema in Pakistan. The book raises the question of whether Pakistan is the result of a "two-nation theory" hastily put together and announced in 1940 as the Lahore Resolution, or has there been a historical separatist urge in the territory we know as the Indus Basin.

Recently, Pakistan lost its most distinguished historian. K.K Aziz believed that like governments, a people get the historians they deserve. In a country of 160 million people, only five or six historians actually wrote and published. And soon this 'failed generation' gets set to pass the state into the hands of an even more hopeless generation. This one opened its eyes under the dreadful rule of Ziaul Haq; when textbooks were mangled to portray Pakistan as a 'besieged state' under threat from a Hindu India, a godless Soviet Union and an anti-Islamic West. The result is now all around us.

Some time back prominent educator Dr Pervez Hoodbhoy had

explained "Most students have not learnt how to think; they cannot speak or write any language well, rarely read newspapers and cannot formulate a coherent argument or manage any significant creative expression. This generation of Pakistanis is intellectually handicapped."

If inquiry and analysis were forbidden for the earlier generation, then the present one may not even have learnt how to construct a question. In such a culture isn't it natural that obscurantist explanations and fundamentalist dogma will take over, conspiracy theories will flourish?

Against this the Jamaat has kept its fundamentalist narrative evergreen and intact, when it says that it is not religion's fault the state of Pakistan hasn't succeeded, it's the fault of the people who never became 'pure Muslims'. Within these wheels are the recruitment networks of the various jihadi outfits — in an environment of multiple social anomalies and economic deprivation — and we are facing a very real spectre of a radicalisation of many of the 93 million Pakistanis who are today under the age of 24. Out of curiosity how many will turn to radicalism to chase the promise of untold pleasures in paradise and how many will actually be seeking to improve their lot in this world?

According to Ali Dayan Hasan of Human Rights Watch, "Pakistan is indeed a failed state. A state that does not have enough self-confidence to take criticism.... A state that feels constrained to legalise bigotry and exclusion, extremism and prejudice, coercion and oppression in order to survive ... [Pakistan] is certainly not presiding over a vibrant, successful and self assured society." If Ali was to travel to the past and meet Jinnah, with this message from the future, what would Jinnah's response be to him? Perhaps more importantly, what would Jinnah's questions be to him? Might one of the questions be "when did you people stop asking questions?"

SLAYING THE DRAGON

On January 4, 2011, Punjab governor Salmaan Taseer was assassinated by a policeman. Mumtaz Qadri was a member of his security detail and accused him of blasphemy. Taseer had only questioned the wisdom behind the law which prescribes death penalty for the offence. The episode was symptomatic of the extent to which religious extremism had come to permeate the Pakistani state and society. Far beyond madressas in the border regions, it extended to the heartland, Punjab, and ominously infected the security forces.

May 2012

AT a quiet lunch recently, a top western diplomat expressed his amazement at the sight of lawyers showering Salmaan Taseer's killer Mumtaz Qadri with rose petals.

"I thought most Pakistanis were Barelvi — moderate Muslims — and the Salafist thinking would not find resonance here. Tell me then," he went on to ask me point-blank, "does Al Qaeda's retributive ideology find resonance with ordinary Pakistanis?"

For a few seconds I was speechless, another diplomat froze, as he held his fork midway to his half-open mouth, all eyes gaping at me. Amidst a tense moment my fleeting mind searched for an answer that would diffuse the tension. "I'll tell you what finds resonance with ordinary Pakistanis your Excellency; Bollywood!" The chuckles around the table told me my retort had done the trick, but several weeks later I still don't have an answer to his question.

"No Pakistani would condone blasphemy," an elderly gentleman proclaimed at a dinner a few days later, a few grains of rice caught in his beard.

This time I was not speechless. "Very well then, would any Pakistani condone taking the law in one's own hands? Would he or she condone an act of cold-blooded murder? Had Salmaan Taseer himself committed any act of blasphemy?" I shot back. The elderly gentleman just shrugged and continued eating, his head down.

A younger fellow sitting next to me leaned in close and lowering his voice suggested "you see it's really all inspired. There are foreign powers backing the Taliban ... all these attacks and bombings, it's all a huge conspiracy".

"Be that as it may," I replied. "What stops our military from liquidating the TTP? Why does it take US drones to eliminate Nek Muhammad, Baitullah Mehsud and others that are locked in war against our military? And if these elements are foreign-backed, shouldn't we hit them twice as hard?"

Talking to my compatriots, I get a sense of utter confusion over what we're dealing with. To further cloud matters, the state institutions are not on the same page. What you get is total dysfunction and strategic paralysis producing little will and determination to decisively deal with a clear and present danger.

Political religion, vigilantism, militancy and terrorism are not individual phenomena but a continuum of the same strain. They function together as one large living creature and this dragon feeds off the society which it inhabits.

Today that society is Pakistan.

In 2008, when Al Qaeda claimed responsibility for the bombing of the Danish embassy in Islamabad in retaliation to some obscure blasphemous cartoons, a series of questions ran through my mind. The last and perhaps most reprehensible in my innermost thoughts was; was Pakistan the only country in which Al Qaeda could find a Danish target?

The project to de-radicalise Pakistan requires a clear road map and a systematic plan to relentlessly pursue precise pre-determined objectives. Containing the TTP alone is not going to serve much purpose unless the whole ecosystem is drained. If you peel off the top layer it regenerates. You have to eliminate it at the core underneath three layers.

Back to my earlier question: to remove the first layer, what will it take for our military to decisively liquidate the Tehrik-i-Taliban Pakistan? Given the recent jailbreak in Bannu, my instinct says the TTP is alive and well.

Down to the second layer, I ask the interior minister and the provincial chief ministers: what is stopping our civilian security agencies and police from liquidating the various jihadi outfits amidst us, the LeT, LeJ and HuM and all those other initials, of which lists are already there? The people are known, their locations are known. Who needs to approve the operation? What resources are needed? If given both, when can we see results?

Coming to the third layer, don't the provincial home departments have precise locations of this infrastructure of global jihad that spawns mosques, madressahs, safe houses, jihadi publications, websites, recruitment and training centres?

Getting to the core, do information and indeed the cognitive capabilities with which we process everyday information play a role? Do the education system and curriculum also need cleaning up? At the same time, isn't it the job of the information ministry to disseminate an intelligent and credible counter-jihadi narrative? Are there merits to regulating the preaching in mosques and madressahs? Should these be brought under the control of the civilian security apparatus of the state?

Can a de-radicalisation project succeed without a meticulous purge within the institutions? Without this, you will hear things like 'by time we got there they had escaped'. Assassin Mumtaz Qadri was an insider. Can we spot others?

Let's be clear, 2014 will bring a substantial reduction in US presence in Afghanistan. It will not bring an end to the war. As the factions fight for the spoils, the war will, in all likelihood, escalate. We must keep that bigger war from spreading inside our territory. That will only be possible if we build internal resilience and deny the use of our territory and prevent our citizens from participating in the coming conflict in any capacity. The US drawdown is an opportunity to extricate ourselves from this conflict.

The present policy flux between the institutions must end. They must come together to develop a coherent and proactive policy that addresses defence, foreign affairs and the economy in an integrated manner. This window of opportunity is still open and the time to slay this dragon has never been more urgent.

WAR WITHOUT END

Many in Pakistan continued to mistakenly believe that a US exit from the region would bring an end to the war. In fact, the real war on terror was only about to begin.

February 2013

THE major point of contention between the Afghan Taliban and International Security Assistance Force (Isaf) is the Taliban's insistence that all foreign forces leave Afghanistan when the drawdown ends in 2014.

Behind this demand in fact lies their fear of airpower. The force they want out more than anything else is the 2,000 airmen. In Afghanistan whoever controls the air enjoys the upper hand.

The Soviets experienced this during the mid-1980s when they brought in helicopter gunships and began to decimate the mujahideen. Within a couple of years the CIA gave the mujahideen Stinger missiles which brought down the Soviet helicopter gunships and cleared the skies. The rest is history. As the Berlin wall came down, Afghanistan had already become some distant corner of the world. Forgotten and isolated, Najibullah's regime with an army of 35,000 still managed to hang on to power for three years. By that record it would appear that the present Afghan government may stand a better chance of staying longer.

The Afghan National Army (ANA) today is over 200,000 strong; in fact never in its history has the country had a standing army of the size as it does today. And though not as cohesive and professional perhaps as the one in the days of the Soviet bloc, this army is better equipped.

As Australian Brigadier Roger Noble, director of operations and plans for Isaf told the Australian Associated Press in Kabul recently: "The Afghan army fights. Their soldiers are brave. They are better than the enemy in most cases."

In addition the Afghan National Police, also trained by Isaf and the National Directorate of Security, which is the intelligence agency patterned on the US Department of Homeland Security, together provide a security infrastructure the like of which has previously not been seen in

Afghanistan. So with this as the starting point, how will the civil war unfold?

In the very unlikely event that the two sides arrive at a truce it will not hold out for long. In fact there are not two sides but when you include the likes of regional warlords Dostum, Ismail Khan, Yunus Qanuni, Fahim et al there are several sides each having contributed thousands of soldiers to the ANA. The remaining 40 per cent of the ANA is made up of Pakhtuns.

Kabul may not face a direct onslaught as it did in Najibullah's time. Formidable airpower will remain in the Bagram airbase and other places like Kandahar, Shindand and Mazar-i-Sharif.

Attack helicopters and fixed-wing aircraft will keep the estimated 25,000 Afghan Taliban from descending on Kabul. The aircraft and surveillance drones will also keep vigil on Pakistani jihadi groups that breach the Durand Line from approaching Kabul from the south or the east.

Kabul residents however remain sceptical of the Afghan security forces' ability to stave off the threat. This is an asymmetric war after all and numbers don't matter because the Taliban don't stand and fight. They attack, and then melt away. At other times they hit with vehicle bombs or roadside improvised explosive devices.

The overarching question really is how quickly the ANA will begin to dissolve. Isaf knows this and to slow down the ANA's inevitable dissolution is also leaving behind 10,000 or so trainers and soldiers that will constitute what are termed 'embedded units' inside ANA detachments. Their job is to boost the ANA units' confidence and capacity to operate independently and to build their morale.

Usually within 12 minutes of Isaf ground patrols coming into contact with the enemy, airpower scrambles to the scene to assist. It is likely that Isaf will continue with this standard when the ANA takes over its functions. The ANA would need to be enabled to coordinate and request an air strike. That role is to be played by the embedded personnel.

Not surprisingly, the Taliban also want them to leave. The Taliban strategy will be to try to crumble morale and accelerate the rate of defections in the ANA. The Taliban will also endeavour to infiltrate the force with a view to increasing "green on blue attacks" on the embedded personnel, which have a devastating effect.

And as long as Nato airpower dominates the Afghan skies the Afghan Taliban and other renegades will seek sanctuary in Pakistan's tribal areas. And as long as there continue to be sanctuaries in Pakistan, the drones will come after them. Likewise, as long as the civil war goes on in Afghanistan,

Pakistani jihadis will find sanctuary in the lawless Pakhtun badlands on the other side of the Durand Line.

Given the mutual interest in each others' territories there is a greater chance that likeminded groups on either side will coalesce.

To pick a line from Mao's Little Red Book, "Political power grows out of the barrel of a gun"; then in these badlands, money comes as an adjunct to political power. As a natural consequence activities including smuggling, drug trade, kidnapping for ransom and criminal syndicates extending to plunder the relatively more prosperous and settled side of the Indus River will intensify.

The other power centre in the region, the Pakistani military, will at best be able to loosely regulate these warlords and every now and then chase away militant groups to the other side of the river and at other times across the Durand Line.

In an atmosphere of mutual mistrust and suspicion and the likely lack of collaboration among the three parties, a beleaguered Pakistani state, the nominal government in Kabul and the US forces holed up inside Bagram, the eventual collapse of the Afghan National Army and remaining security infrastructure is inevitable.

Vast swathes of a fragmenting countryside would fall to powerful warlords as the entire region reverts to its default historical setting: the western periphery of the Indian subcontinent, between the Oxus and the Indus that Babar would have encountered when he first arrived in this region at the beginning of the 16th century.

DON'T TALK, FIGHT

By early 2013, Pakistani security forces had cleared all the settled areas of NWFP (now renamed the Khyber Pakhtunkhwa province) and six of the seven tribal agencies from Taliban control. The military appeared reluctant to venture into North Waziristan. Major General Athar Abbas, who was then military spokesman has now said that detailed plans for a military operation had been drawn up as early as 2011 but the then Army Chief, General Kayani was reluctant to move ahead. The main reason though may have been the Pakistani military's ambivalence to fully give up its double game that had been played since 9/11. Meanwhile the militants, both foreign and local were lodged in North Waziristan which was the scene of numerous strikes by US predator drones. The coalition government comprising the PPP, ANP and MQM favoured use of force against the extremists. When insurgencies are put down they fold back and resort to terror tactics. Their aim is to break morale. Pakistan was struck with a wave of terror attacks, assassinations and suicide bombings; many of which appeared to originate from North Waziristan. As elections approached, once again voices began to be raised calling for negotiations with the Taliban.

March 2013

NAWAZ Sharif was recently heard saying that if the Americans can talk to the Taliban in Afghanistan then why can't Pakistan talk to the TTP?

Political leaders that adopt this line of reasoning betray a limited understanding of how the world works. The American constitution, their civil rights and the American way of life is not being negotiated in Nato's backchannel talks with the Afghan Taliban. Not long ago the Taliban was the de facto regime in Afghanistan. Nato may see some merits in co-opting them back into the power structure in Kabul.

Let's get one fact straight. The Americans are not in Afghanistan to defeat the Taliban. They are not there to occupy or stabilise or rebuild that country. Regardless of the motives that misinformed conspiracy theorists in this country may attribute to them, the Americans are in Afghanistan (together with the military contingents of 40 other countries) to ensure that Al Qaeda and its affiliates are rendered incapable of launching spectacular attacks against the US (and other countries).

Since September 2001, there has not been an attack like the one on USS Cole, or like the ones on the US embassies in Kenya and Tanzania, much less like 9/11 itself. It would seem that the US military is delivering on at least one key objective. This is what Congress has authorised it to do and has agreed to pay for it, over the years, with $700 billion of American taxpayers' money.

As it withdraws from Afghanistan, the US will leave behind an elaborate intelligence apparatus as well as precision strike capability in the region. This is a long way from 1998 when the US Navy fired (and misfired) Tomahawk cruise missiles — from warships at sea — aimed at Al Qaeda bases in Afghanistan (and Sudan).

Today it has a bevy of choices — among which armed drones, fixed wing aircraft, Navy SEALs and attack helicopters — with which to ensure that extremist religious forces based in this region do not raise their head again and strike at targets worldwide.

Now the calculus of achieving a complex objective like that may involve negotiating with the Afghan Taliban. What the Taliban may hear from Nato at the negotiating table would be this: 'Back in October 2001, you were asked to hand over Bin Laden. You ruled Kabul then. We not only got Bin Laden but most of the top Al Qaeda leadership as well. You however, no longer rule Kabul.'

From this posture they may go on to offer the Taliban a back door into Kabul. Set a thief to catch a thief goes the old dictum; and so the Afghan Taliban in return would have to hold out an assurance that foreign, jihadi and extremist forces will not use sanctuaries in the Pakhtun areas of Afghanistan to stage spectacular attacks against the United States.

There may be other quid pro quo offered to the Taliban. Last week Al Jazeera reported that Afghan President Hamid Karzai had sent a message through Norwegian interlocutors to the Taliban in which he offered them the ministry of justice and the position of chief justice. It is conceivable that the Taliban will ask, and Karzai will agree to let the Taliban's moral police operate in the Pakhtun areas of Afghanistan with powers to scrutinise people's lifestyles and appearances and to punish offenders.

To understand what the Taliban want one only has to look at the Kunar province in Afghanistan where they rule. "Democracy and western ideas of women's rights are against Islam," the regional Afghan Taliban commander tells Al Jazeera and "there can be no alternative to Sharia, which is God's law". Meanwhile the footage shows squads of the vice and virtue police at a checkpoint, one turbaned official holding a cane and half a dozen others, armed with assault rifles, hooded and wearing balaclavas, checking cars to make sure they don't have music players and that cellphones do not have cameras and video footage.

Kunar is also the hiding hole of Mullah Fazlullah and his Swat Taliban who escaped Operation Rah-i-Raast in Swat in 2009. From Kunar, every now and then they will sneak across into Bajaur Agency and from there into the mouth of the Swat valley where they force the closure of schools. Last October Mullah Fazlullah's gunmen barged into a school bus. They asked for a student who they identified by name to stand up otherwise all of them would be shot. A 14-year-old girl stood up and took the bullet to her head. Her name is Malala Yousufzai.

The refusal to acknowledge the existence of the Punjabi Taliban has created a security bubble in Punjab, and whilst the province may have been "spared" it continues to sit on a sectarian volcano. You cannot endlessly sweep things under the carpet.

Pakistan is home to the world's largest jihadi infrastructure (and there are many more Mumtaz Qadris within the Punjab police). This factory of jihad needs to be systematically dismantled. Such things do not happen without force. The longer we delay, the more protracted and bloodier it will be. It is like delaying an operation for fear of surgical pain. Things get more complicated.

In 2007 an extremist assassinated Punjab's minister for social welfare, Zil-e-Huma in Gujranwala. A little while later there was an assassination attempt on interior minister Aftab Sherpao. The operation against Lal Masjid followed and there were widespread retaliatory attacks across the country. Yet Benazir Bhutto chose to return that year. Elections were held in 2008.

Politicians that are fearful of, or complicit with, the extremist religious forces are Pakistan's Achilles heel. This is the time to stand up and fight. Running away from this war is no longer an option.

RUMOURS AND CONSPIRACY THEORIES

Most societies, past and present have held certain dogmas. In Pakistan a further aggravating cause is that instead of scientific reasoning and rational argument, its educational environment fosters rote learning. The effect is high conductivity (to borrow a term from electricity) of rumours and conspiracy theories. Where they shape public opinion or where they get reinforced into dogma, their prevalence becomes a major impediment to solving problems.

March 2013

WASN'T the Soviet invasion of Afghanistan said to have been about our warm waters? Never mind whether it was the Cold War or Charlie Wilson's war, wasn't there the obscure theory that the USSR, not having maritime access commensurate with its superpower status, must be after the Balochistan coastline?

They never came for it, nor has anything been found in declassified documents or in scholarly literature to lend credence to that fantastic hypothesis. In 1979, armed men seized the Grand Mosque at Mecca. Even in those innocuous times, who but the Americans could have been behind it? Within hours, a mob had razed the US embassy in Islamabad to the ground. Turned out, it wasn't the Americans at all but Saudi Arabia's domestic politics.

The early 1990s was a terrible period of ethnic and criminal violence in Karachi. Spurred by migration from tribal and rural up-country regions, the scramble for Karachi's living spaces had begun. Talk began to be heard about a sinister plan to detach Karachi from the rest of Pakistan.

After Hong Kong reverts to communist China in 1997, the Western banks and businesses there would need an alternate haven, went the conspiratorial claim. And even as it was causing a speculative spree on Karachi's property market, the theory failed to take into account Chinese leader Deng Xiaoping's experiment with market capitalism and the special economic zones that had started as far back as 1980. It also did not explain who was seeking Karachi, to the preclusion of better Asian candidate cities, as an alternative to Hong Kong.

Who carried out the 9/11 attacks? Well, Jews, of course.

How did this theory originate? A story in the internet edition of the Jerusalem Post of Sept 12 of that year mentioned that the Israeli foreign ministry was collecting the names of 4,000 Israelis believed to have been in the areas of the World Trade Centre and the Pentagon at the time of the attacks. By the time a Jordanian paper ran its own story, Israelis had been interchanged with Jewish Americans and "unaccounted for" had been lost in translation to mean not having shown up for work. That squared the circle — they knew in advance, proof they're responsible.

As human beings we carry simplified representations of reality in our heads which form our beliefs and preconceptions. Encountering a phenomenon in conflict with these preconceptions becomes a cause of tension and discomfort. In psychology this is referred to as cognitive dissonance.

How can Muslims have done this in the name of Islam? Either we modify the belief to accommodate the new facts or — if the fuse doesn't blow, the appliance will — our judgment about that phenomenon becomes distorted. This irons out the discomfort and allows people to continue to hold on to their beliefs even in the face of overwhelming evidence to the contrary.

A major motivation for the propagator of the conspiracy theory is the sense of importance it brings. "Why do you think Nato is in Afghanistan?" The propagator will lean forward and, lowering their voice, give you the inside scoop: "Afghanistan has $1 trillion of mineral wealth."

Never mind the fact that America does not have much of a primary commodities processing industry that could make use of this supposed mineral wealth. China does, but then assuming that if anybody wanted ores and minerals from Afghanistan, wouldn't it be simpler to follow the commercial route in which one of the companies can go in and negotiate a mining lease?

In some ways a conspiracy theory is akin to the concept of a scapegoat: a convenient and intellectually lazy way to shift blame for one's own predicament — it's not our fault, it's them! Extreme forms can take on mass psychosis, of the type that gripped Nazi Germany in the years leading up to World War II.

Who killed Benazir Bhutto? Zardari obviously.

Why would he want to do that? (Leave alone how he could manage that in General Musharraf's Pakistan.)

"So that he could take over the party and become the country's president," quickly comes the retort.

To believe this, one has to take not one but several leaps of faith, one after the other. The first bet is that within weeks of BB's death, the dictator-general would honour his pledge to hold elections. Suppose Musharraf had reneged, and locked up Zardari for murder? What was plan B? The second bet is on the outcome of elections 2008 being different from 2002. Who was to say that with Benazir gone, the PPP would not split up into factions? Who knew with certainty that it would instead go on to win against the king's party? Then, in the next act, the military strongman has to become a strawman and resign. Finally, Zardari has to get elected as president, which he does eventually — and through a consensus in broad daylight, not by conspiracy. But then comes a huge anticlimax: having got there, he strips himself of all powers.

Sounds bizarre? Conspiracy theories are. Here's another one:

Perturbed by the population bomb of anti-American and radicalising youth in Pakistan, Western intelligence agencies are collecting data through tracking the social media, closed-circuit television footage of attendances at rallies and activity at polling booths. Unwittingly, Pied Piper Imran Khan — playing the tune on the wrong side of the war — is serving as an invaluable sieve. After the dust settles and everyone's gone home, there will be extensive lists, identified using facial recognition technology, of security risks for Western countries. Millions of names collected thus would be sent to Western embassies in Islamabad to be barred from travel, visas, admissions, jobs or scholarships. In the end, the war will be won using biometrics and data processing.

DIGITAL SNOOPING

Even as I may have ended my last article "Rumours and Conspiracy Theories" in jest, I chose to develop the theme further, if only to illustrate how communications intercepts, biometrics and data processing could be deployed even by Pakistan as viable tools to fight the war on terror.

January 2014

IMAGINE viewing the digital log of your daily life. Your day started with the alarm going off on your smart phone. You squinted at the text message from the boss informing you about shifting of the meeting venue. As you were brushing your teeth you flicked the city traffic channel on your digital set top box. As you drove to work, your GPS tracked the route you took. Your debit card has logged the time of your coffee break downstairs.

Among other such mundane items, your day's digital log also contains your browsing history (even though you took care to delete it from your computer), the Google searches you conducted and all those who called you.

Broadband internet was introduced 14 years ago. Smart phones followed a few years later. Then came 3G and now with 4G, the slope of the technology curve — and rate of innovation — keeps getting steeper. And with that, the rate of diffusion of new devices and applications has become mind-numbing. Each time you log in, download, view a photo, you are leaving a digital fingerprint. What many of us may not realise is how commercially valuable this data is.

Today technology companies are positioning themselves for what will be the grand finale of all marketing battles. Unlike the past when customer numbers and market share were contested, the coming battle is about whose operating system emerges dominant i.e. whose rules everyone else will play by. Google, Apple, Microsoft and Facebook are the frontrunners in a race. The 'also ran' list includes IBM, Hewlett Packard and Bell Labs (UNIX) who have now fallen behind.

What is certain is that operating systems will gradually eclipse more and more of our lives. An increasing range of items and gadgets — which may include cars, kitchen appliances, home-lighting, even eyeglasses that can self-adjust in shade and power — are going to run on operating systems in future.

What these companies are vying for is not simply to become the master of one box or one device, but to become the operating system of our lives. That will be a position from which they can manage, monitor (and ultimately monetise parts of) the data flow of everything we do.

Google reads your emails before you do, technically that is, when its robots crawl through the content and serves up ads that it thinks are most relevant to the content of the message.

But it appears your daily digital log has more than just commercial value. Whistleblower Edward Snowden gave us a glimpse of how the US National Security Agency (NSA) has been hacking into servers to collect whatever it could lay its hands on. From breaking into the computer network of Brazil's state-run oil company Petrobras, to monitoring German Chancellor Angela Merkel's mobile phone, to sweeping up millions of French telephone records.

The documents Snowden passed onto the Guardian and the Washington Post also describe a secret project called PRISM, which is the cover name for collection of user data from Google, Yahoo, Microsoft, Apple and five other US-based companies.

Because obtaining this data directly from the servers of the Silicon Valley giants would involve cumbersome US legal procedures, the NSA (and its British counterpart) under another project code named MUSCULAR is pirating telephone traffic and internet data from interception points — that are outside US jurisdiction — such as undersea fibre optic cables.

Once acquired, the raw data is dumped into NSA's massive data centre in Utah. The documents show that Pakistan is one of the two countries (Iran being the other) from which the largest amount of data has been taken in. Quite surely, US spooks have been listening in to Al Qaeda chatter as well as keeping an eye out for a nuclear warhead going astray.

If what Snowden informs us is correct, then all your and my daily digital logs for the past several years may be available with NSA. As NSA's robots crawl through the data, they look for any unusual pattern. So for example, if you were using a disposable mobile phone and switching on only long enough to make brief calls and afterwards switching off the phone, then that pattern would certainly mark you for special scrutiny. As technology improves, NSA would doubtless also be able to predict future behaviour and emerging patterns. Given the already hysterical levels of anti American frenzy in this country, it is important to remain steady when digesting this information. With the copious amount of data it has collected, NSA's search engines and crawlers can pull out the digital log on any target — politician, government official, diplomat or private citizen. And whereas an "arms race" with NSA cannot be won, not even by Google, a complete review of our government and military communications procedures would be in order.

WRONG AGAIN

The spring of 2013 found Pakistan in the midst of its election campaign to elect a new government. Barack Obama had been re-elected for his second term. The US surge in Afghanistan had ended but violence levels hadn't decreased. A drawdown of troops was underway. US predator drones were targeting Taliban sanctuaries in North Waziristan, from where the US believed a lot of the attacks on Coalition forces would originate.

April 2013

Imran Khan got it wrong again – for the umpteenth time. The PTI manifesto unveiled recently proposes to pull Pakistan out of the US' war and everyone lives happily ever after. By this time I'm actually beginning to wonder why no one in Khan Sahib's party appears to have a voice to talk him out of presenting a fairy-tale solution to the county's most serious issue – fighting religious extremism.

When he says "extricate from America's war", then how does one walk that phrase? Do you end the alliance with the US? As a policy prescription that's fair enough, as long as the pros and cons of that have been thought through and it is not simply being presented as a rhetorical solution. Or does extrication simply imply not letting the remaining Nato supplies transit through Pakistan. (Incidentally Nato now relies less on Pakistan and more on the northern supply route). Or does it mean pulling out our forces from Fata and letting the Taliban and other foreign renegade groups find sanctuary in a region where they feel safe because it is outside the reach of Nato's air power? But then has the manifesto thought about the consequences of leaving a vacuum in Fata? Does it understand how hot pursuit works and when it becomes permissible under international law? Has it evaluated the risk and consequences of that region being used as a base to launch attacks on the Afghan side of the Durand Line?

Or let's take the drone war, [Imran] Khan Sahib's favourite whipping boy. If evidence emerges of a militant compound on a hillside in Orakzai agency, do we undertake that airstrike ourselves? Or do we send in ground forces? In either case, whose fight would this be? But supposing we don't act. We refuse to fight the war on anybody's terms. What would the probable Nato response be? And finally when the drone does come, what do we do? Do we engage it with our own air power? What could be the reprisal of doing that and how far are we prepared and equipped to let that spiral escalate?

Good security policy is built on scenarios. Scenarios are not predictions – far from it – they are often nightmares we hope we never have to see. But a proactive national security policy has to foresee all possibilities – however unpleasant – and script out responses to deal with every eventuality. You cannot have an incompetent "Ah we never thought of that..." type of response.

Here's another scenario for Pakistan Tehreek-e-Insaf and Khan Sahib's team to mull over. It's 2016 and you are in power. There has been a terrorist attack on the US. There are unmentionable casualties. Evidence is rapidly emerging that the attack is postmarked from Pakistan. Some group has handled the Pakistan end of the operation. The American public is baying for blood. Western embassies are evacuating their personnel from Islamabad. Foreign airlines have suspended operations. Our Embassy in Washington informs you that the CIA has provided its list of 250 suspected terrorist sanctuaries in Pakistan – safe houses, training camps, compounds, and radical madressahs – to the American president. Never mind that the list is somewhat outdated, as long as it can be acted upon to satiate the American public.

Inside the Situation Room, President Obama is presiding over a meeting of his entire national security team – reviewing plans for precision strikes against these 250 targets. Meanwhile, Khan Sahib's erstwhile colleagues and companions from the Difa-e-Pakistan Council are burning tyres and effigies of Obama and from the Mall roads of Lahore, Rawalpindi and Peshawar, threatening more attacks on US interests worldwide if the Americans retaliate against the terrorist attack.

End of nightmare and start of reality. The PTI needs to identify a list of actions that can be taken today and demonstrate how these will minimise the risk of such a scenario. As it begins to flesh these out, it will come to the realisation that there is more than one war that needs to be fought. While we are fighting terrorism we are also fighting a Taliban insurgency. While a counterterrorism strategy and a counterinsurgency strategy may have areas of overlap, one predominantly utilises intelligence agencies, while the other uses Special Forces.

The PTI also needs to show how it intends to defeat the ideology(ies) of religious extremism, and how it proposes to dismantle the infrastructure of jihad in central Punjab. For now, unfortunately, the

Tehreek-e-Insaf has produced a wrong prognosis of the situation and shown an even poorer understanding of the affliction. You cannot come to power with half-baked and muddle-headed ideas, only armed with hope and good intentions.

In more jumbled confusion the PTI manifesto paints the nationalist armed struggle in Balochistan with the same brush as the war against religious extremism. Devolution under the 18th Amendment followed by the NFC award has started to extinguish the fires of separatism in Balochistan. The credit for that goes to the recent PPP-led coalition government and to all the parties that were part of the last National Assembly. More recently the army chief and the chief election commissioner have both visited Quetta to convince all parties there to take part in the elections. The Baloch problem is being substantially addressed – and not by rhetoric alone.

Meanwhile it's important for Khan Sahib to get the fight against religious extremism right. To begin with, there are people within his party he can listen to.

DEFINING TERRORISM

Even as the PML N government, that had assumed power after winning elections, pursued negotiations with the Pakistani Taliban, it began to overhaul the legal framework to fight terror. To this day however, Pakistan does not have a consensus definition of terrorism, and there is widespread confusion within both state and society; indeed the concept is poorly understood by many.

October 2013

October 2013

SO it appears the government is putting in place legislation intended to give state authority the upper hand against terrorist violence. Among other things, it will empower officials of the state security apparatus to act decisively and with necessary authority against threats of terrorist violence. This is a step in the right direction but only just a step in a 1,000-mile journey.

That terrorism is a contested concept is best illustrated by that old adage; one man's terrorist is another's freedom fighter. There is no generally accepted definition, and often the question of defining who is a terrorist becomes linked with the issue of de-legitimisation of certain groups and their politics. Therefore, without a working definition of terrorism, further powers for the security apparatus are prone to abuse. The label of 'terrorist' needs to be applied judiciously otherwise it risks becoming devalued and ultimately 'demonetised'.

Three elementary concepts may help us build a more meaningful definition. 1) Terrorists are not 'crazy' nor are they solely the poor and dispossessed. 2) Often the direct targets are not the main target, the main target are those who continue to live. 3) Terrorists want a lot of people watching, not necessarily a lot of people dead. Abhorrent as they are, extortion, kidnapping and homicide are criminal, not terrorist acts.

For better vision and clarity we would need to un-bundle the criminal and separatist violence in Karachi and parts of Balochistan respectively and place them outside the realm of terrorism. Widespread confusion also continues to prevail as to the real threat that seeks at best, to change the character of the state and at worst, to destroy it.

Terrorism and, by extension, vigilantism, militancy, sectarian violence and violence against minorities are the different manifestations of the same ideological urge. At terrorism's core lie the basic questions that are crying out to be dealt with. Who is an apostate in Islam? Can the state ascribe such a label to any citizen or group? Indeed, can one citizen or group label another citizen or group as kafir? And if it does, how should the state respond. What is the takfiri movement and how can a modern state like Pakistan restrain its violent urge? Do the present laws and enforcement mechanisms provide sufficient restraint? What is Salafi ideology and who are the Salafists in our society? What do they believe in and what do they preach? Has a census been conducted on their mosques and madressahs?

What are Al Qaeda's ideological grievances and how does the organisation justify the use of violence to redress these? Why does this line of reasoning find traction amongst so many ordinary Pakistanis that are not yet radicalised, but can potentially become cannon fodder with very little effort? The Pakistani state must wake up to this ticking time bomb. Psychologists say that the human mind has a primitive ego defence mechanism that negates all realities that produce too much stress for the brain to handle. It's called denial.

When we look around, we find the public and political discourse in Pakistan on such questions to be of very poor quality. Academic discourse is almost nonexistent. On any given day, one would seldom hear parliament taking up such questions. A case in point is the argument that acts of terrorism are a cause of drone strikes against militant hideouts. This is half-witted hearsay. There is no empirical evidence to support this contention or establish a causal connection.

To survey the post 9/11 work that has been done on understanding the causes, mechanisms and processes of terrorism I typed in "causes of terrorism" in Google Scholar. Gleaning through the first eight mind-boggling pages of search results you notice something.

Cutting edge work has been done and when you look at all the big names, the scholars, universities, think tanks and research institutes, the academic journals and the publications, and then you plot these results on a map, you notice that almost all this effort has come from the West, concentrated on both sides of the Atlantic.

You can find the odd twinkle in Israel, Singapore and Australia, while the rest of the world is fairly dark. Yet Western researchers decry the data being scattered, and the difficulty of gathering it from conflict zones. That the environment is ever changing. That intelligence agencies and terrorist organisations are shadowy and accessing people to interview is a challenge. Even if the researcher can gain access, they try to influence the researcher instead of assisting the research effort.

One piece stands out: Jessica Stern's Terror in the Name of God: Why Religious Militants Kill. A leading expert of terrorism, Dr Stern teaches at Harvard's Kennedy School of Government. One of the reviews described her work as unusual because she is a trained social scientist who spent four years collecting primary data, in which she had first-hand contact with suspected terrorists, even if at great risk to her own life.

Usually one would find intelligence operatives or journalists in such roles but rarely somebody of her background and expertise. She finds religious terrorists to be the most dangerous in the world today. Her work is a gem, offering insights that get us to the heart of the matter in very little time. It should be required reading for our policymakers and security planners.

The study of terrorism (and its countering) brings multiple disciplines together. For the greater part the subject falls under political science but its study involves an understanding of war studies, communication studies, social psychology, criminology and law. The 1000-mile journey will require much more rigorous thinking and a far greater intellectual effort than has been managed so far. But for now, coining a definition for terrorism is the next step.

FAZLULLAH'S WAR

After Pakistani Taliban leader Hakimullah Mehsud was killed in a US drone strike, Fazlullah replaced him as the new leader. He had earlier carried out a brutal attack on the Pakistani military, beheading 17 soldiers. Then in October 2012 he had ordered the assassination of schoolgirl activist Malala Yousufzai. To protest the drone strike that killed Baitullah Mesud, Imran Khan ordered party cadres to block trucks carrying supplies for US and coalition forces fighting in Afghanistan. And even as Pakistan's government and right wing parties clamoured for talks with the Taliban, Fazlullah assassinated an army General in a bomb attack. The same month, General Raheel Shareef assumed command of the Pakistan Army.

November 2013

Shortly after 9/11, when the US bombing campaign had begun in Afghanistan, a force comprising 8,000 fighters from NWFP crossed the Durand line, hoping to find and kill American soldiers. Many were barefoot, some were as young as 16. Several were carrying little more than knives and spears and axes with which they intended to wage their jihad. It wasn't long before they were in the captivity of the Northern Alliance.

This primitive force was drawn from the cadres of the Tehreek-e-Nifaz-e-Shariat-e-Muhammadi (TNSM), an obscure militant organisation with limited nuisance value, whose head Sufi Muhammad had long been campaigning for Islamic law in Swat and Malakand. Successive Pakistani governments were guilty of sweeping the issue under the carpet and leaving it to simmer. Nine years and a radical transformation later, this force would engage the Pakistan Army in the longest battle of its history – Operation Rah-e-Raast.

The leadership for this transformation came from Mullah Fazlullah, Sufi Muhammad's son-in-law. His transformative strategy centred around three broad initiatives: 1) deploy FM transmitters across the region to wage a propaganda war and win the narrative; 2) recruit and indoctrinate fresh talent; and 3) train this talent in guerrilla warfare for which Fazlullah reached out to Baitullah Mehsud who promptly sent across a contingent of foreign fighters from Waziristan – Arabs, Uzbeks and Chechens – to do the necessary.

This track record notwithstanding, Fazlullah remains a 'non-Mehsud outsider'. As such he would be looking to prove his mettle and demonstrate some early successes. A spike in violence with some high-profile attacks is predicted in the coming weeks. In these we can expect the security forces and other symbols of state authority to be targeted. Fazlullah is aware that hitting targets in Punjab would raise his stature among the Mehsud militants. His strong link with Al-Qaeda, which already has local affiliates and operatives in Punjab, makes such an undertaking quite feasible.

Judging from his Swat experience, Fazlullah recognises the value of propaganda as a weapon. As a terrorist group wins people over to its cause, its strength increases exponentially. Many may actually agree with the terrorists' objective even if they have reservations about their tactics. Others may feel that, in the circumstances, even the grisly tactics are justified. Fazlullah probably recognises that the TTP has not fully milked this potential and many more can be brought round to the TTP's point of view.

In this, Fazlullah's job is made easier by large overlap between his rhetoric and that of the PTI and radical members of the Difah-e-Pakistan Council (DPC). Simply put, the rhetoric goes: "The government of Pakistan is a slave to the United States ..." The difference of nuance being that Fazlullah's second part of that proposition states "...and is therefore a legitimate target for attack" while the PTI and DPC's second part of the proposition states "Nato supply lines must be shut".

Many who fall in the grey area in between these two may agree with a third proposition which states that "attacks on Nato forces in Afghanistan are legitimate". It is in this triangular space, bound by these three propositions where the battle is being waged for the hearts and minds of millions of those Pakistanis who stand at the threshold of becoming radicalised. It is here where Fazlullah would be seeking to pick up maximum gains.

Where Mehsud and his clan may have felt that enough impact and fear had been created to sit down with the government and realise some of the political gains, Fazlullah and his clan clearly have a different view. Why cash the chips when you're on a winning streak? Between now and when the US withdraws from Afghanistan next year, why not gain even more strength and bring the Pakistani state to its knees? You can extract bigger concessions that way.

A possible demand could include Pakistan's demilitarisation not just from Fata, but from all the territory to the west of the Indus. In the meantime Fazlullah is likely to relocate the TTP's power centre from the Mehsud region to Afghanistan's Kunar and Nuristan region, beyond the reach of the Pakistani military. This would give the TTP strategic depth and multiply its strength by building linkages with Afghan commanders and warlords on the other side of the Durand line.

The paradox of terrorism is that, on the one hand, tactical success does create impact, while on the other, the civilian casualties alienate the local population which is often counterproductive to political goals. There are already signs that terror attacks will shift from civilian to military/ political targets. From the perspective of the rebels this raises their prestige to warriors instead of terrorists and 'legitimises' the violence in the sense that there are now 'two sides' engaging in warfare instead of one side killing civilians.

One of the things Fazlullah has learnt from Al-Qaeda is how to use jihadi jingoism to undermine the morale of the security forces; and to create dissent among the ranks. The Jamaat-e-Islami, through the recent statement of its ameer, has already laid the foundation on which to build on. Finally, Fazlullah would also seek to integrate with the Punjabi Taliban and sectarian jihadi groups to build inroads into the 'enemy's' heartland.

As the government dithers on action, the PTI and religious parties are busy filling their pockets with the political capital they acquire from drumming up anti-west hysteria. The liberal political parties have already been marginalised. The security establishment awaits a change in guard. Meanwhile the clock ticks as the date for Nato's withdrawal from Afghanistan approaches. The window of opportunity for Pakistan is fast closing.

WHAT'S THE PLAN?

Terror is a potent weapon. It is an asymmetric tactic of an ideological group to meet its larger objective. The TTP is a coalition of ideologically similar but disparate groups. Some seek to destroy the state; others to seize it while yet others to influence it using forceful means. The range of terror tactics sought to break the morale of the citizens. And they were working. By the winter of 2013, the government of Nawaz Sharif was coming under increasing pressure to bring an end the violence. And Pakistan entered talks with the Taliban. On the other side, the government of President Hamid Karzai was also holding secret negotiations with the Afghan Taliban. The essence of power is to be able to influence the actions of your adversary. The Taliban had done just that; and to the world outside, appeared to be winning the war in both Pakistan and Afghanistan.

February 2014

EVEN when times get as bad as this, there are a few things that don't worry me. I am not worried that we face a formidable challenger in the TTP, which is lodged in an even more challenging terrain. Neither am I worried that any military operation here will push their fighters into Afghanistan.

I'm not in denial, yet it doesn't worry me that heavily armed Taliban groups now sit on the outskirts of Karachi or that they can direct events inside the city from their suburban nests. I am also not worried that assorted jihadi groups and their sympathisers are embedded within our urban centres and even infest our state institutions.

I am also able to shrug off the reality that half of the Coalition forces have already left Afghanistan and by December the remaining would also be gone. At the back of my mind I also know that there will be no reconciliation between the Afghan government and the Taliban. I am aware that this will mean that conditions will worsen in the Pakhtun areas of Afghanistan and that a further two million refugees can be expected to arrive.

I am also not excessively worried about the growing extremism in our society. It is a difficult situation, I am aware, but it is not the difficult situation that worries me.

What worries me is that there does not appear to be a plan. What worries me is that the government, the rulers and the civilian institutions of the state are not seized of how deep this cancer is. What worries me is the absence of clear thinking, and of a credible road map that proposes to chart a course out of this difficult situation.

Giving peace a chance? I will not spend time arguing with generic clichés. But 'peace' is not merely the absence of violence. Except in the international relations theory of deterrence — of balance of power — where heavily armed states will not go to war for fear of mutually assured destruction.

In the context of individual nation states, peace is said to prevail when the rule of law prevails, when the writ of the state is supreme and when the state holds a monopoly over violence. Our conditions are far from this. Neither are these conditions likely to result from the current negotiations.

Nobody expects these talks to lead anywhere or to yield any information — about TTP's demands, its whereabouts, or its fault lines — that was not already known. On the other hand the talks have accorded a degree of legitimacy to a terrorist group and to its toxic 'cause'. They have provided it a platform on nightly prime time television to disseminate poisonous narratives. Putting this genie back in the bottle may not be as easy.

I have reasonable certainty that there will soon be a series of military operations against TTP groups. How will these be qualitatively different from previous operations? How effective would they be and how precisely will they target the enemy? How will TTP fighters be prevented from fleeing to Afghanistan? What is the plan to capture those who do slip across the Durand Line? Is the necessary coordination being done with Nato and the Afghan security forces? Are there enterprising warlords on the other side who may be up for a bounty hunt? And indeed how does the military address widespread concerns about the efficacy of its conventional forces fighting an asymmetric war?

Considering that the cost of failure may be nearly as high as the cost of inaction, we can only gain from seeking more clarity on such questions. This clarity will also instil more confidence in the public — part of which is still sceptical about the military option.

Even then, any military operation in Fata will address only part of the problem. The other part lies in the settled areas and in the cities where very little pre-emptive action is presently visible. A case in point is Karachi where, in the ongoing operation being conducted by multiple provincial and federal agencies, only 60-70 Taliban fighters have been arrested in the last six months. It is hoped that together with the main bastion in Fata, a simultaneous and broad sweep will scoop up all the snake pits in the cities.

There is also the question of resourcing the war. The budgetary allocations are still not visible. In such a situation, who will take any plan seriously? A good plan, it is said, is like a road map. It shows the final destination and the best way to get you there. And a good plan today is better than a perfect plan tomorrow.

CONTOURS OF THE THREAT

In February 2014 the TTP Mohmand, one of the extreme radical groups within the alliance beheaded 23 soldiers of the Pakistan army whom it had been holding in captivity. The next day Pakistan's air force jets bombed the group's hideouts. Soon thereafter the talks resumed again.

March 2014

THE only certainty one can be sure of, they say, is change. And even as we look into an uncertain future, we can see some key trends. Then we look at the forces that are driving those trends and slowly a pattern begins to emerge. These visions make the future look less hazy. Here's some of what we see:

Pakistan is facing a long war and this is not a war that will produce a victor and a vanquished anytime soon.

Pakistan is fighting a creed. This war is not so much with the Taliban as much as against the Talibanisation of our society — the Tehreek-i-Taliban Pakistan (TTP) representing only the extreme end in that spectrum.

The right-wing narrative is beginning to sound more and more ludicrous. False premises — that this is 'America's war', that drone strikes are a key cause of terrorism and the Taliban are 'misguided brothers' — led to flawed prescriptions: block Nato supplies and negotiate with the Taliban. That narrative may well be at risk of becoming unhinged. It is difficult to decide which is more outrageous: Interior Minister Chaudhry Nisar suggesting a 'cricket match with the Taliban'; or Pakistan Tehreek-i-Insaf chief Imran Khan suggesting that the majority of Taliban are 'peace-loving' and the TTP therefore should be allowed to open an office in Peshawar.

The relatively liberal parties are displaying clearer thinking, and a realisation that they may have a story that will better resonate with their constituencies. Expect them to keep churning the wheel to their advantage.

The parties of the right, arranged like dominoes, cannot stray too far from their long-held positions without appearing to be 'switching sides'.

Eventually if they do come round, they will find themselves in a squeeze zone, encroaching on the turf of the liberal parties whose story would be more original and spun to a greater degree of sophistication.

A continuous low to medium intensity conflict is foreseen. This is the 'steady state' that the talk-fight-talk-fight sequence appears to be heading towards.

The TTP will mostly strike military targets. The TTP as an Al Qaeda affiliate has been tutored in propaganda by the likes of Abu Yahya al Libi, Al Qaeda's erstwhile chief information officer. Al-Libi was killed by a predator drone but not before he taught the current TTP chief Mullah Fazlullah that attacking military targets will raise the militants' prestige without greatly alienating the right-wing civilian population. Only when a strong message needs to be sent to the civilian leadership will the TTP strike a civilian or political target.

The 'cat and mouse' game will continue without a decisive outcome. The TTP fighters will escape into Afghanistan when the fighting season ends or if they come under unbearable heat. Other fighters may melt away into the plains and settled areas and remain hidden for a while. This way, the TTP will pose a continuous and sustained challenge. Some factions seek to destroy the state and military, others seek to unravel it through breakdown and desertions and yet others, notably the TTP Mohmand, wish to seize the state intact. Quite likely that some factions will at times break ranks. Meanwhile, on its part, the military has already demonstrated its newer methods and technology and we can expect to see increasing sophistication in surveillance and targeting in the months and years ahead.

Right-wing and religious forces will harness the TTP threat to their advantage and insert themselves as interlocutors in the process. From this position they can leverage their strength and extract maximum concessions from a beleaguered state. As the TTP held the gun to our heads, the Council of Islamic Ideology was recently able to put pressure on us to change laws restricting polygamy and child marriages.

The situation ironically places liberal parties in an enviable position giving them an opportunity to craft a more sensible and sellable narrative with which to win back followers lost to the right.

To contain any such successful thrust from the liberal parties, the TTP will use the threat of violence as it did in the general election last year when it did not allow them to campaign or hold political rallies.

Pakistan will remain part of Al Qaeda's larger battlefield which includes Afghanistan, Iraq, Syria, Yemen, North Africa and parts of

Central Asia. The TTP will not only draw 'franchise benefits' but also fully leverage the 'strategic depth' available to it in Afghanistan's Pakhtun territories.

This may yet be a simplified model but one that lets us construct more elaborate scenarios with these building blocks. Such scenarios can help us gain an understanding of the shape of things to come and hopefully prepare pre-emptive policy responses.

THE
MIDDLE EAST FACTOR

AL QAEDA & THE PROTEST MOVEMENT IN ISLAM

Al Qaeda is a late 20th Century incarnation of radical Islam. Its genesis owes to a unique set of circumstances but what is more relevant is its globalizing impact. Most of this is owed to its meticulous propaganda team which could give a clever and deviant spin to what may have been popular misgivings. It would then eloquently articulate 'causes' to orchestrate unifying support from widespread radical Islamist groups. Finally it would direct their wrath to bring about spectacular attacks on targets across the world theatre. Nevertheless, the organisation's conception remained poorly understood by most Pakistanis most of whom are not familiar with Muslim political thought, Arab nationalism and 20th century events in the Arab world.

June 2009

For Abdullah Azzam, that day in 1967 must have been the most impressionable of his life — from the hills overlooking the West Bank village of Jenin, white flags signifying surrender going up on the rooftops of houses, tucked in between palm trees and olive groves ... the Israeli army moving in.

Azzam a young man, fought this — six-day — war with Israel, which in fact was a 24-hour walkover as the Arab armies abandoned their defences and their air forces were crippled on the ground. The defeat was total.

For Azzam and many across the Arab world, the 1967 defeat triggered painful soul-searching. A vast amount of literature came to be produced by Arab thinkers, writers and intellectuals in search of 'where did we go wrong'. Many began to term Gamal Abdel Nasser's 11-year quest for Arab unity a failure. The Arabs not just lost the war and territory, they also lost faith in their leaders, their countries and in themselves. As happens in times like these, some looked towards redefinition; others looked towards various forms of protest. Even while Nasser's prisons held 28,000 Islamists, mosque loudspeakers started blaring that Islam was the answer.

The earliest form of protest in Islam came in the form of the Kharijite (those who went out) movement in the seventh century that posed the first serious challenge to Caliph Ali. The Kharijite doctrine took one step forward by Ibn Taymiya's introduction of the term 'takfir' in the 14th century. The verb is derived from the Arabic root 'kufr'(heresy). Whereas the noun, 'kafir' refers to the infidel, takfir refers to the process of excommunication. Once takfir is admitted as a legitimate concept in political thought, it brings us to Alice in Wonderland's allegorical 'fork in the road', one side of which leads to deviant doctrines.

In the 19th century pan-Islamist thinker Jamal ud Din Afghani while directing his anger at western imperialist domination also, from the corner of his eye, was addressing authoritarian Muslim rulers. Muhammad Ibn Abd Al Wahhab in the 18th century and Hasan Al Banna in the 20th century introduced fundamentalist movements in Islam.

The emphasis was on the need to 'cleanse' society of corrupt influences. Afghani, Wahhab and Banna all agreed on the need to replace weak rulers and states with strong ones. Unlike Taimiya they however remained ambivalent about sanctioning violence against Muslims.

In modern times, the term is most associated with Sayyid Qutb who was a strong advocate of takfir as an instrument to protect Muslim society. He was also influenced by his contemporary, Abul Aala Maududi, who argued that social and economic justice were, in fact, the ultimate benchmarks that Muslim society ought to set for itself. Combining the takfiri and Maududi doctrines, Qutb insisted on the need to first purify society of 'the vulgar influences of the West' only after which it could set benchmarks to achieve social and economic justice. He also explicitly sanctioned the use of violence and jihad against fellow Muslims. The ends justify the means, he argued. Shortly afterwards, Qutb was hanged by Nasser's regime on a charge of sedition.

Now, the mosques, in protest to the humiliating defeat against Israel, were raising his name once again. Whilst the Muslim Brotherhood in Egypt stood for political participation, Qutb's followers began to invoke the ancient Islamic doctrine of 'hijra', which is a reference to the group's withdrawal from what it considers a pagan society. Taken together 'takfir wal hijra' came to symbolise an innovative doctrine whereby a group would withdraw from what it considers heretical Muslim society in order to build its strength in isolation, and then strike back once it has achieved sufficient strength. The gates of violence and jihad against Muslims were finally declared open. More recently, Al Qaeda's use of the Arabic term 'qaaidun' which approximately translates to 'fence-sitters' has added further sophistry to this line of reasoning by suggesting that within a 'heretical' Muslim society these elements must either be brought into the jihadi fold, or, if they stray too far, eliminated.

As a youth, Osama Bin Laden watched with wide eyed-admiration the 1979 seizure of the Grand Mosque at Makkah by Juhayman's Saudi group that was protesting against a 'corrupt and tyrannical monarchy'. He heard Khomeini give a voice to Qutb's writings as he turned his wrath on 'a corrupt West' and an 'infidel' Baathist Saddam Hussein. Bin Laden observed Arab nationalism crumble and give way to a rigid theocracy which now defined an Islamist agenda. As a student at the King Abdul Aziz University in Jeddah he studied under an Islamic scholar who had a doctorate from the Al Azhar University in Islamic jurisprudence. His name was Abdullah Azzam and he hailed from the West Bank town of Jenin.

The Cairo Citadel, built by Salahuddin al Ayubi, sits on a hill overlooking the Cairo of the Fatimid and Ottoman periods. In its dungeouns are the prisons where Islamist suspects are brought for questioning by the police. Ayman al Zawahiri spent three years here inside a stone cell; perhaps four feet by eight — after Islamists assassinated Sadat in 1981 in protest for signing a peace treaty with Israel. It was here also that he met 'the blind sheikh', Omar Abdul Rahman — who had been a professor of theology at Al Azhar University. According to Rahman, the declaration of jihad needed a fatwa to justify actions that would otherwise be considered criminal. Many believe that the tragedy that visited America on Sept 11, 2001 was born in the prisons of Egypt.

The exact date of the conception of Al Qaeda is a subject of debate. But the plot bears a striking resemblance to Clint Eastwood's epic, The Good, the Bad and the Ugly. Bin Laden had the money, Azzam the ideas and Zawahiri the organisation ... three men representing different worlds coming together to fight the Red army in Afghanistan.

Towards the end of the war, Azzam — who 20 years earlier had seen Jenin surrender to the Israeli army without a fight — finally felt he was now ready to settle scores. He wanted the Arab legion to relocate to fight 'the real war' ... against Israeli occupation. During the first Palestinian Intifada which started the previous year in 1987, Azzam had helped establish Hamas as a protest, an alternative to the PLO which was considered too secular. Bin Laden and Zawahiri however had other plans. In a final standoff between the three, Azzam was assassinated outside his home in Peshawar by a car bomb. It was by 1989 that a deviant ideology was beginning to turn into a revolt.

THE FUTURE
OF THE MIDDLE EAST

The Arab Spring uprisings were perhaps the most significant event in the region since the end of the Ottoman Empire. A lot of bottled anger that had been kept contained by authoritarian regimes was being released on the streets. As regime after regime faced the people's wrath, not only did they respond differently but events in each country took a turn in a different and quite unpredictable direction. Now against that backdrop, Pakistan, with its nascent democracy and freedoms appeared robust and resilient.

February 2011

OUR campus lay on the other side of Tahrir Square — from the now burnt-out headquarters of the Egyptian Democratic Party on the Nile corniche. During the peak of Mubarak's power, I was a young student at the American University in Cairo; in an Egypt that was a bastion of order and stability.

While outside, Tahrir Square was being dug up to make way for the Cairo underground metro, a symbol of the regime's prestige, inside, above the loud thudding of the piling machinery, Prof Tarek Ismael would explain the foreign policy behaviour of Arab states by drawing typologies on the blackboard.

"The swathe of territory across North Africa, Mesopotamia and Arabia has been carved out into a series of states with artificial borders." He would draw two by two matrices to explain that among these successors to the Ottoman pre-system, there were rich states and poor states, there were capitalist and socialist development models and there were regimes threatening to the West and regimes that were allies of the West. However, despite differing orientations, one common strand ran through all of them: authoritarian regimes ruled by autocrats.

The Cairo metro was inaugurated, I graduated with my degree in Middle East politics and subsequently a $100 bn in foreign aid and investment have poured into Egypt. Two decades later, Mubarak's regime is tottering but Prof Ismael's hypotheses stand even more robust. And when people ask me whether the scenes witnessed on the streets of Cairo would indicate similar vulnerability elsewhere in the region, I am tempted to return to his frame of reference to construct my answer.

True to form, the present unrest has hit poor states — Tunisia, Egypt, Jordan, Yemen and Sudan — that had long pursued the capitalist development model. On the other side of the Red Sea, do the rich states such as Saudi Arabia and others in the GCC have cause for anxiety? With the enormous resources and reserves at their disposal, surely they can throw more money at the problem. But generous public spending is seldom a substitute for political expression and inclusion.

Kuwait with a parliament and Qatar with Al Jazeera TV began experimenting with limited political freedoms, some years ago. Suddenly much more is needed and much faster to keep this flood out. Even with these, some level of domestic disturbances can be expected in the months to come.

The 40 per cent of Egyptians living below the two-dollar-a-day poverty line are not the ones converging on Tahrir Square. Instead, it's the students and young educated unemployed and white-collar middle class galvanised by social media like Facebook. Meanwhile, many Cairo taxi drivers and small shopkeepers have lamented the protests which have deprived them of daily earnings.

Similarly, the peasantry appears aloof from the protests or mildly in favour of the Mubarak regime. So is it really economic hardship or the demand for political freedom that is driving the protesters? For the moment the anger appears directed against the ruling party and the state as is evident by the burning down of the party headquarters, of police stations and by the attack on the information ministry and state television, while the worst wrath is reserved for the person of Hosni Mubarak who for most Egyptians is a symbol of repression and tyranny.

Accordingly the chant of the protesters was 'Freedom'. These features of the uprising would indicate that Saudi Arabia and the other rich GCC states on the capitalist model may not be that immune after all.

On the other hand, the rich states that adopted socialist development models, Iraq, Libya and Algeria would be relatively less affected and may have the longest time to begin reform. Their prosperity and relatively better social structure may serve as shock-absorbers. Still, their political systems would need to become less clogged — as has Iraq's after Saddam

Hussein.

Predictably, their response would be to strengthen their welfare state models and move towards greater political freedom. Of course, a Middle Eastern perestroika carries inherent risks. Algeria, which started this process over 20 years ago, was soon confronting an Islamist rebellion.

Nonetheless, the risks of not acting are greater.

Whether the regimes embrace change or have change forced upon them will depend on how well they 'get it' and how fast they act. When he uttered remarks in support of Mubarak on the fifth day of protests, the Saudi king obviously didn't get it. Mubarak himself didn't get it when he offered the proposition of "security for Egypt" while the protesters demanded freedom. Neither does the Jordanian monarch get it when he sacks the government and appoints an army general as prime minister.

Five years of reform undertaken by the Egyptian regime's technocrats, $45bn in foreign direct investment and 3.5 million jobs later, the grievances still remain. It is difficult to imagine how more such reforms would be any more effective. Nevertheless, now that the genie of people's power is out of the bottle and on the streets of cities across the Arab world, there are many scenarios going forward. Here powerful forces like Arab nationalism, a common language and culture, the role of Islam and the question of Palestine ensure regional cohesion and threaten potential systemic contagion.

What is certain is that order and stability are bygones and change is the new buzzword. Israel gets that — and we can expect it to remain ahead of the curve. I only got a 'B' in Prof Ismael's course but America, like the slow learner, has stayed behind the curve. Probably a C minus for that.

EGYPT: RISKS & BLUNDERS

Even though most Pakistanis are devoutly Muslim and the Islamist parties are allowed to freely participate in the political process, paradoxically, political Islam was never quite able to acquire much traction in the country's political system except during periods of military rule under Zia in the 1980's and Musharaf in the early 2000's. In contrast, the situation in post Arab spring Egypt, was unfolding rather differently.

August 2013

What were the Egyptian generals thinking when they went in for the heavy-handed crackdown on the Muslim Brotherhood? That with enough force you could get the protesters off the streets and deter them from coming out again? That with sweeping emergency powers they could round up the Muslim Brotherhood's core members and their families? That the Brotherhood would drop the protests and maybe even quit politics?

The crackdown may have been a tactical mistake. Vice President ElBaradei's resignation is enough to suggest that the generals did not seek counsel from civilian or political leaders. Hawks in the 'Deep State' are calling the shots in Cairo.

The Muslim Brotherhood knows that the longer it can keep the demonstrators on the streets, the more sympathy and legitimacy it can build for its cause. The more repression the regime responds with, the more international ire and condemnation it will draw – and in the process isolate itself. Gamal Abdel Nasser had also severely repressed the Muslim Brotherhood. His prisons held 28,000 Islamists. But then Nasser espoused an anti-imperialist grand narrative, built on Arab nationalism and the Non-Aligned Movement. At the time the region too was dominated by authoritarian but secular regimes in Syria, Jordan and Iraq, which collectively suppressed political Islam. Meanwhile Yasser Arafat's PLO – in its wisdom – also chose not to raise the flag of religion to galvanise support for the Palestinian cause.

The humiliating defeat in the 1967 war with Israel changed all that. Nasser's narrative lost traction. Mosque loudspeakers across the Arab world started blaring that Islam was the answer.

Several radical and Islamist groups emerged and chose violence rather than participation. The Brotherhood, founded in 1928, has continued to disavow violence and pursue participatory politics. Even then Nasser's successors, Anwar El Sadat and Hosni Mubarak just about tolerated the Brotherhood, and kept it at the fringes of the political system.

It is one thing to disenfranchise a political ideology as under Nasser, or to rig elections and steal victory as under Sadat and Mubarak. It is quite another to annul a legitimate political mandate after it has been acquired through an electoral process. And it is politically naive to paint a political party that has won elections as terrorists; or to expect it to wind up and disappear. So what are the major risk scenarios going forward?

The Muslim Brotherhood presently does not have a militant wing. If the repression continues, there is a risk of radicalisation within its rank and file. Hamas, its ideological ally in Gaza, could become the most likely source of weapons, as could state sponsors. Then there are other Egyptian Salafist jihadist groups, with no stakes in electoral politics. Most of these would like to instigate violence and create an environment in which they can flourish.

Gaza is linked to Sinai via underground tunnels, which serve as conduits for infiltration and weapons supply for Hamas. In Sinai itself, an insurgency against the Egyptian security forces is underway and there have been rocket attacks across, into the Israeli port city of Eilat on the Red Sea. Such activity can invite pre-emptive and retributive strikes from Israel turning Sinai into a flashpoint.

In the assessment of officials of the US Defence Department, the Egyptian military is not a viable fighting force. Its capability to conduct counterinsurgency operations is even more limited. There is little doubt that Al-Qaeda and its affiliated radical Islamist factions will be trying to infiltrate the protests and turn them violent. It could also promote attacks on state institutions and Coptic institutions to further polarise the conflict and draw the state into retaliating.

The risk of spiralling violence is, therefore, very real. That would squeeze the space for the Muslim Brotherhood and force it to reconsider its policy of non-violence. And while the Brotherhood has been careful not to change the status quo on the peace treaty with Israel, a major unsettling could force it to review that stance.

As in Syria, many others would have interests in Egypt, and stakes in the outcome of the conflict. The risk of a proxy war breaking out is also very real. Behind the scenes, positions are already being drawn and scenarios being fleshed out by regional players, notably Iran and the

Hezbollah. For the US, the security of the state of Israel is the vital interest. International shipping would be anxious about potential disruption to the Suez Canal.

Meanwhile, Arab states would be apprehensive about the ripple effect the conflict would create and the extent to which that can disrupt their existing security matrix. Paradoxically for example, both Saudi Arabia and Israel would find themselves on the same side in this conflict; this may have domestic implications in Saudi Arabia.

Political Islam, no matter how undesirable, cannot be wished away or swept under the carpet. As in a boxing match, the best way to deal with it is to bring it into the ring, which is the metaphor for the political system, and defeat it there. Egypt's generals seem to have done the opposite. After last month's coup, this was their second tactical error.

SYRIAN CALCULATIONS

In particular, events in Syria took a particularly ugly turn. While on the hand Assad's regime refused to capitulate, on the other the rebellion against it came to be led by radical Islamist groups. Major regional players were involved in a proxy war and everybody's stakes were high. This protracted conflict with no end in sight was looking to become a poisoned well for the whole region.

September 2013

THE international community appears polarised over the issue of attacking Syria. This is not the first time the Syrian regime has allegedly used chemical weapons against the rebels. Since the conflict began in March 2011 chemical weapons have reportedly been used on a few occasions, though on a smaller scale. Saddam Hussein too had gotten away with using them, during the Iran-Iraq war and later, against the Kurds.

These weapons are banned by international convention, though Damascus is not a signatory. In any case, despotic regimes will have few qualms about using them — as tactical terror tools — to put down rebellions that threaten their existence. How freely they use them will depend on how far they can get away with it.

Terrible as they are, these weapons work in two ways: they spread panic in enemy ranks, and devastate morale as its fighters abandon the battlefront to rush to their families and support bases against which such weapons are usually launched. Secondly, they remind other rebellious communities of the consequences of rebellion.

Increasingly grisly tactics have been used by both sides in this war. The Assad regime has bombed populated areas using helicopter gunships, aircraft and even scud missiles. It has used cluster munitions and now the US administration has concluded "with high confidence" that Bashar al-Assad has used chemical weapons. On their part, the rebels calling themselves the 'Free Syrian Army' have carried out suicide bombings and executions of the regime's collaborators.

The fighting in the Syrian civil war is concentrated around three well-populated regions: Damascus in the south, Homs and Latakia near the Mediterranean coast and Aleppo, Syria's largest city near the border with

Turkey.

So on this particular occasion, what could the regime's generals have been trying to accomplish with chemical weapons? The rebels' recent acquisition of shoulder-fired surface-to-air missiles had unnerved the Syrian regime. The rebels could threaten the regime's helicopters and aircraft, including civil aviation, and Assad probably was going to take no chances with tolerating them in the capital.

Iran had sent the Lebanese Hezbollah to help Assad's forces beat out the rebels from Damascus. One suburban region was, however, proving to be a hard nut to crack. The logic of the hawks in the regime probably went as follows: let's take a drastic measure to eliminate this clear and present danger. We will deal with any international outcry later. It will also tell us how far we can push the envelope across Obama's 'red line'. If it gets discovered, we'll deny involvement and cloud the matter.

We will also delay the UN inspectors from reaching the site and use the window of time to erase the evidence. This will substantially weaken America's moral leverage for a strike. In this window, we would have cleared Damascus of this existential threat.

This is sound war logic. But if it cleared Damascus of one threat wouldn't it create the bigger threat of a US strike? Not really. In the regime's calculations, this perhaps was a reasonable trade off. US strikes would only inflict limited damage, on known targets. Even then, to minimise losses some of the assets could be moved out. Any military hardware that got destroyed could be replaced by Russia, which maintains two military bases and several military advisors in Syria.

The regime correctly assessed that if the US struck, it would not take matters to a tipping point where rebel groups could gain a decisive advantage. The US would have to walk a thin line. The gravity of the scenario — with nightmarish implications for Israel's security — is not lost on the US in which foreign fighters of the Al Qaeda-linked Al Nusra group get hold of chunks of Syria's stockpile of chemical weapons, which is one of the largest in the world.

Additionally for Russia and Iran, regime change in Syria would be a red line. Therefore the US strikes, if they came would be clinical, not lethal. The Assad regime also calculated that if the rebels got their hands on anti-tank weapons then they would only be one final and lethal push away from Damascus. Therefore this beach head had to go, even if it was going to take chemical weapons and embracing the risk of a US punitive strike.

There was another payoff. America attacking yet another Arab country would trigger outrage across the Arab world. This wave would tap into the sentiment of populations of Arab countries, most of whose governments are inimical to Bashar al-Assad. It would serve as the Syrian regime's fifth column of sorts and create political difficulties for several Arab governments that cheered the bombing. Meanwhile Assad would gain stature as the defiant Arab leader who stood up to the West.

So what are the Assad regime's options? Syria can likely absorb a US strike as long as it remains symbolic and from which it can create political capital. If the US does not strike, then that too suits the regime fine. Either way, it is hard to rule out the possibility of his regime again using deadly weapons — which remain at its disposal.

If, in the unlikely event the strike is somewhat harder than a rap on the knuckles, the risk of the Syrian military taking aim at the Israeli-occupied and annexed Golan Heights, provoking Israel to retaliate cannot be ignored. Nothing would flare sentiment on the Arab street faster than an armed conflict with Israel. If the stage comes where Israel is provoked into responding, then a Rubicon would have been crossed in the present stand-off. The conflict could then spiral beyond anybody's ability to control. And that must be avoided at all costs.

PLAYING WITH FIRE

April 2014

TO diagnose Saudi Arabia's fear instincts, one would have to travel back to 1979. That year saw the Iranian revolution, and Ayatollah Khomeini's subsequent talk of 'exporting' the revolution which has left Saudi Arabia with an exaggerated fear of Shia expansionism.

That same year, hundreds of armed extremists seized the Grand Mosque at Makkah. Shortly afterwards, two brigades, roughly 10,000 Pakistani troops, were deployed to Saudi Arabia under a bilateral joint military agreement aimed at protecting the Saudi monarchy.

One part of Saudi Arabia's anxiety stems from its perception of a growing Shia footprint which now includes the Bashar al Assad regime in Syria, the Hezbollah militia's strength in Lebanon, the Maliki government in Iraq, and the three years of Shia led pro-democracy protests in Bahrain.

Saudi Arabia is also suspicious of its own Shia population in the Eastern Province, where it fears the radical Hezbollah al-Hejaz is active.

At the same time, it is nervous about any domestic unrest that may be inspired by the Arab Spring uprisings. This nervousness was apparent when it announced a generous financial support package for its own population in 2011.

It is particularly wary of the mobilising capacity of the Muslim Brotherhood, whose political Islamism and grassroots activism are anathema to the House of Saud, whose grip on power comes from keeping religion under its own tight control and patronage.

And even as Egypt's military junta has ousted the Brotherhood's government (and received billions of dollars in Saudi largesse), it has stoked much Islamist resentment in the Arab world.

In the clearest sign of this fear, Saudi Arabia has recently declared the Brotherhood as a terrorist organisation and passed new anti-terror laws that Amnesty International regards as a tool to crush peaceful expression.

Saudi Arabia also faces a radical Islamist threat from Al Qaeda in the Arabian Peninsula which is now lodged in Yemen. It is entirely plausible that AQAP has been making every effort to penetrate Saudi Arabia's state institutions and security forces.

Saudi Arabia promoted the Syrian rebellion against Bashar al Assad.

That proxy war has reached a stalemate. The rebellion has been hijacked by jihadist groups who have turned on each other.

The fighting is out of anybody's control and now Riyadh fears the fire may spread. Many Saudi fighters who had joined the rebellion could become the link between underground Saudi Islamist groups and jihadist groups fighting in Syria. In a royal decree announced last month, Saudi Arabia has banned its citizens from participating in the Syrian civil war.

A prolonged conflict in Syria could also spill over into Egypt where an Islamist movement against the military junta is in early stages. That would further complicate the Kingdom's threat matrix.

The recent quiet sidelining of Prince Bandar bin Sultan, head of Saudi intelligence (and the mastermind of the campaign to overthrow Assad), is the clearest sign of this reordering of threat priorities. He is no longer to be in charge of Saudi policy on Syria which will now be handled by Interior Minister Prince Mohamad bin Nayef. Nayef's skill set? Counterterrorism work against Al Qaeda.

Saudi Arabia may yearn for an early end to the war and the establishment of a transitional government in Syria, but is this objective realistic? Would Assad's ouster necessarily end this war? Are the Russians going to stand by and watch the demise of their only ally in the Arab world? How will they likely respond to anti-Assad rebels receiving shoulder-fired anti-tank and anti-aircraft (and possibly even heavier) weapons, that Pakistan has been showcasing at its IDEAS defence exhibitions?

How will Iran respond as these weapons arrive in Jordan for subsequent issuance to selected rebel groups? There may well be an end user agreement; but do we really intend to monitor and enforce it? Are our trainers and other mercenaries also expected to arrive in Syria? And as the situation further complicates, will our friends in the Gulf expect other quid pro quo?

Some reports indicate that the Saudis are considering a standby force ready to put down Islamist and Shia uprisings whenever and wherever they may appear in the Gulf.

Such questions need to be pondered by our policymakers before further entangling us in this crisis. The parliament is the forum for such debates and policy appraisals.

Our representatives may also want to revisit the reasons why recently the US had hesitated to arm the rebels. They may similarly want to evaluate other risks and repercussions of this engagement. It's time to open the windows and let in that fresh air.

FIGHTING ISIS

Just as a unique set of circumstances had earlier given rise to Al Qaeda, now new ones had combined to create ISIS. Of course the new scenario now held implications far beyond Syria and Iraq. For Pakistan too; the ramifications were significant considering it was fighting a battle for its own survival against Salafi and sectarian extremism. Yet the World had no coherent strategy on how to tackle this new monster.

February 2015

LAST week a group of retired US generals warned Congress that by disengaging from the region, the US may lose the war against extremists. This is sound advice that President Obama may have heard before.

The US is leaving the region more unstable and less secure than it was before its military interventions in Afghanistan and Iraq. And while for Pakistan and Afghanistan, stability and security will now largely depend on how well the Ashraf Ghani administration and Pakistan's security establishment are able to work together, it is Iraq and Syria where the situation is far more complicated. Only the US as the sole superpower can help resolve this dreadful mess. And more than military power or 'nation building programmes', this may be more a job for US diplomacy.

The full-fledged 'Sunni' rebellion that Iraq faces today is no less a consequence of premature US disengagement as it is of former prime minister Nouri al-Maliki's misrule who made sure to completely disenfranchise Iraq's Sunni population. Building on this disaffection, the Islamic State has overrun the Sunni regions where the Iraqi army units defected without a fight, leaving behind vast arsenals. It has established a 'caliphate', a totalitarian 'state', over territory larger than Jordan. The perfect storm that created IS would not have been possible without the Syrian civil war, which affords it much strategic depth.

IS has galvanised Salafist fighters and funds from across the world. It has begun to spread its influence to distant Libya and Yemen. It is not strictly an insurgency but a 'state' building organisation, whose military council includes well-trained former officers of Saddam Hussain's disbanded army and intelligence services.

On the other hand, the response against the group has been a patchwork of uncoordinated actions rather than a unified strategy put up by the states of the region. Iraq, Syria, Saudi Arabia, Iran and Turkey, the Kurdish peshmerga militia as well as Russia and countries of Western Europe have divergent interests and mutual mistrust. They are unable to act against this formidable fighting force or check the flow of motivated fighters and its sources of funds. Their national intelligence agencies rarely share information or collaborate. Meanwhile IS has threatened retaliatory attacks if the West gets in its way. Amidst this response paralysis the organisation thrives and grows.

Yet there is a silver lining. The Islamic State is a common threat to all players. It has no state backing; at least not just yet. And this may provide an opening from where US diplomacy could pick up the thread.

Perhaps the most debilitating obstruction to coining a joint strategy is the Saudi-Iranian rivalry; a religious rivalry that extends deep into the vault of Islamic history. The key here lies with the powerful establishments on both sides. A Byzantine challenge for US diplomacy, the Gordian knot as it were, would be to facilitate a détente.

The Islamic State is inimical to the interests of both Iran and Saudi Arabia, to a larger extent than they are to each other. A US-brokered Faustian bargain between these two establishments will leave their respective regimes with more latitude to work with each other towards the common objective. As no less a byproduct it would stall the production of toxic sectarian ferment and bring a windfall to the entire region, especially Pakistan, one of the world's largest sectarian hotbeds.

The other hugely complicating factor is the Syrian civil war. Russia and Iran will not let the Assad regime in Syria fall anytime soon. And nobody wants to contemplate the mayhem that, in the event, will see extremist factions scrambling for power.

The second best option is for the US, working with Russia and Iran to force President Assad's hand to widen his regime, maybe even to the extent of a national reconciliation government. In return, he can get two things. A lowered intensity of rebellion against his regime and co-option into the coalition on the war against IS.

Granted, these are staggeringly difficult diplomatic objectives. But with these two big-ticket items in place, the others — precision aerial strikes, Special Forces ground operations, choking the sources of external funds, preventing the recruitment and flow of fighters into the region and undertaking state building — would be relatively easy.

This is not a job the US can get done alone. Washington will serve its own interests by addressing the region's fault lines and align a broad coalition of states to act together. The war against IS cannot be won by coalition airstrikes alone. Even if the Islamic State unravels, it will go back to insurgency mode. And unless the difficult diplomatic challenges are taken on, the group will keep winning and the apprehensions of the former generals may well prove right.

TRANSIT CORRIDORS & REGIONAL CONNECTIVITY

For decades, Pakistan squandered its advantages bestowed on it by its geography. This section explores certain themes on the topic and what amends can be made.

TIME TO TRADE WITH INDIA

August, 2010

THE return flight from Bangkok crosses Indian airspace flying low over the physical boundary on the final descent into Lahore.

Unlike the Swiss-German border or indeed even the border at Torkham, there is no line of parked cars, buses and trucks, waiting patiently for customs formalities. Instead, one sees a concertina wire fence complete with searchlights, watchtowers and motion sensors.

Before I folded the meal table I had been drawing three overlapping circles, one each representing South Asia, Central Asia and West Asia — or call it the Middle East. The region where the three circles overlap was Pakistan … an enviable strategic position indeed! The finality of being fenced out would appear to indicate one less circle.

Meanwhile I had folded the drawing paper and was now using it as a bookmark placed inside my in-flight read; Imtiaz Gul's The Most Dangerous Place: Pakistan's Lawless Frontier resting in the seat pocket in front of me.

"What Pakistan faces today is not a ragtag army comprised of just a few thousand religious zealots," writes Gul, who also runs the Centre for Research and Security Studies in Islamabad. "Beyond a doubt, the TTP [Taliban] is out to destroy the entire Pakistani security establishment. This will be possible only if the security forces face a continuous and sustained challenge all over the border regions, where one-fourth of the Pakistan Army is now deployed. One thing is clear: a long, bloody struggle lies ahead."

And whilst the mess in Afghanistan may or may not have been influenced by our own blinkered strategic vision, even after 14 years, the supposed trucks from Torkham crossing the Oxus into Central Asia remain a mirage. Effectively, this brings us to only one strategic circle, the Middle East. Even there for the last two decades, Pakistan as a locked state with an impoverished economy has had little to offer (other than a pool of semi-skilled labour).

Judging from the shopping bags my fellow passengers have stuffed in the overhead cabin compartments, it is apparent that not just the Middle Eastern market but Pakistani consumers themselves now demand quality and standards. Accordingly, the last remaining circle, too, fades away. This leaves only Af-Pak. So how do you squander a huge strategic geopolitical advantage? Easy! Hold firm to a flawed strategic vision that is underpinned by an even more flawed ideology — that sees strategic depth to the west and an enemy to the east. How does one change this endemic condition? One way is with economics.

Since 9/11, Pakistan has lobbied for greater market access for its textile products to the US market. "What benefit will this bring?" asked the US administration. "Five-fold increase in exports — from $3bn to $15bn," responded the Pakistani textile industry; a verbal attestation without any economics research to back it up with.

Ten million new jobs thus created would water down religious militancy, a favourably inclined US administration pleads to a reluctant US Congress. "Well, also please do tell us who will bear the cost: US industry and taxpayers or the other textile-producing Asian countries?" asks the US Congress. Once again, without rigorous quantitative analysis these questions cannot be answered and so the issue of free-market access continues to languish.

The gravity model for trade is an econometric estimation technique to simulate trade volume flows between two countries (or two regions). In similar fashion to a war game exercise, it churns out predictions based on input parameters such as the distance between and the relative sizes of the two economies. This technique has been used to predict the outcomes of trade agreements like Nafta (North American Free Trade Agreement).

According to our own logic, Pakistan needs a big market for its export, one that will stabilise the shattered economy. For 10 years we have chased the US market but have missed seeing the huge market next door that even the US and the rest of the world vie for. This is because even while India may have the world's 10th most regressive trading regime it is still the world's second or third most sought after business destination on account of the size and growth rate of its consumer market.

India offered Pakistan the most-favoured nation status, a position any other country would bend over backwards to obtain. Pakistan has yet to reciprocate. The Gravity Model has been applied several times to simulate trade between the two countries under varying assumptions. On average, it has indicated a twenty-fold increase — from the present $2bn to $40bn in two-way trade. This implies a doubling of exports in one stroke. It also implies a cheaper total import bill.

In what may be a competitive model to Singapore, the Malaysian province of Penang is positioning itself to become a regional economic powerhouse. In this scheme of things, Penang's greater economy would incorporate southern Thailand and the Indonesian island of Sumatra. All will benefit. In similar fashion, Lahore, together with central Punjab, stands to gain immensely as a potential hub of a greater economy.

From a geopolitical perspective, the Indian cities of Amritsar, Jullunder, Ludhiana and Patiala are closer to Lahore, (and to Punjab's golden triangle comprising the manufacturing clusters of Gujranwala, Gujrat and Sialkot) than to northern Indian industrial cities in Uttar Pradesh, Bihar or Bengal. Generally for the Indian states of East Punjab, Haryana and Himachal Pradesh, Lahore is the nearest commercial hub and Karachi is the nearest seaport and there is a plausible rail link in between.

The GHQ probably realises that a flooded Pakistan, facing an existential threat emanating from its lawless tribal frontier is also a country with diminished economic war potential to ward off this threat. There is nothing unusual about a policy reappraisal following a calamity. In that sense, the opening of Wagah represents the decisive round in the battle between the forces of progress and the forces of reaction. The choice of moment for that showdown has never been more urgent.

THE NEED TO OPEN BILATERAL INVESTMENT WITH INDIA

April 2012

In a giant leap forward, India has indicated it will welcome investment from Pakistan. As with trade, Pakistani fears on capital flight are unfounded. Instead, Pakistan desparately needs FDI to grow its economy and reduce poverty. Pakistan can seek this FDI from India.

India's savings and investment rates are 37% and 36% of GDP respectively. These two factors alone – which are unlikely to change – almost guarantee India a 7% GDP growth rate. Against this, Pakistan's savings and investment rates are 13% and 14.6% of GDP respectively. These rates stunt GDP growth rate to a maximum of 4%. Energy and security constriants further depress this figure to around 3%.

In the six months between April – September 2011 alone, Indian outbound investment in overseas markets amounted to $ 25 billion. The question we should be asking is what sectors should be opened up to attract FDI from India? In short, I would suggest coal based power generation, steelmaking, IT and software and agro processing sectors.

GOODWILL STRATEGY

May 2012

I have to admit, I never got this "strategic depth" thing. In my experience, strategic depth denotes an arena in which you can retreat to, trading space for time as your adversary advances. From my reading of history, Russia could choose a scorched earth policy against the German invasion in 1941– Moscow and the economic centres are situated well inside the Russian hinterland. It let the Germans stretch their supply lines which the partisans subsequently attacked till the Russian winter bogged down the German army. In our case where the population and economic assets are situated in a narrow corridor bound by the Indus River on one side and the Indian boundary on the other, how would this retreat work? I'm afraid, when meticulously interrogated, I have found "strategic depth" to be an imposter.

Below this inelegant construct in fact lies our insecurity surrounding the Durand line. Afghanistan was the only country in the UN system to not recognize Pakistan. Successive Afghan governments refused to recognize the Durand line. Then, in 1994 came our opportunity to even up. Mullah Omar, leading an obscure force calling itself the Taliban, punished an Afghan warlord to hanging for the rape of two minor girls. The body was left for two days, strung up from the gun of a tank. Mullah Omar became an instant hero and Pakistan dumped Gulbuddin Hekmatyar . It wasn't long before ISI's operatives penetrated Mullah Omar's force. Based on a quick gap analysis this ragtag force was reinforced with madrassa trained cadres from Pakistan. Next the Taliban were trained in mobile guerilla warfare and equipped with 4 by 4 pickups with mounted missile launchers.

Within two years, Afghanistan was over run.

Now came the time for the Pakistanis to cash the investment. True to Afghan style, Mullah Omar refused to accept the Durand line. Neither could Pakistani trucks roll across to Central Asia nor indeed could the gas pipeline from Turkmenistan be stretched across. It was clear that Pakistan's investment had gone sour. Then came Bamiyan. Pakistan pleaded on behalf of the civilized world to spare Afghanistan's pre Islamic heritage. As this world heritage site was defaced with explosive, it became apparent that Pakistan had no leverage with the Taliban.

So much for strategic depth.

After being expelled from Sudan, it was Al Qaeda that instead found strategic space in Taliban controlled Afghanistan. It was from here that the organisation orchestrated the bombings of the US embassies in East Africa in 1998. Once again Pakistan was caught completely clueless when Centcom chief General Anthony Zinni, over lunch in Peshawar informed the Pakistan army chief that US Tomahawk missiles were, at that moment, over-flighting Pakistan on way to targets in Jalalabad.

At the end of the day, strategy only has one purpose: to open up strategic space. On the other hand, our parochial and single track approach appears to have delivered the exact opposite: Closed options for us and created space for others.

Then came 9/11.

As Kabul fell to the Northern Alliance and Pakistan made the U-turn its options further diminished. So today with all options closed what are we left with? Pushed into the corner, our poor excuse of a "strategy" today is this: Preserve the Haqqani network and other renegade "assets" to unleash them on Kabul once the ISAF forces leave.

Let's try to approach strategic depth from the economic prism. Military force is at best one ingredient of a strategy. At the present time and with the tools available, where would one start building a new strategy roadmap? Bringing the Gwadar port into operation perhaps represents the best starting point. The economic utility of this port multiplies if a railway is put up to Kandahar and Afghan trade is allowed to flourish. A flourishing trade route creates economic opportunities; it will provide a stake in peace and stability to the Baloch youth that is today agitating for want of opportunity. When coupled with our own Reko Dik copper deposit and Afghanistan's anticipated $ 700 b iron ore and copper deposits located inside a $ 12b economy, the whole endeavour is a strategists dream to create an electric effect.

Let's also modify the jargon – strategic depth with strategic access. To reinforce this strategic access, the Pakistani NGO sector could have been encouraged to develop farm to market access for agriculture products, extend microfinance and technical skills and integrate these to markets and trade activities in Pakistan. In the 1990's Western businessmen who wanted to do business with China would find a conduit through Hong Kong. At a more modest level, conduits for international mining, construction, agriculture and energy interests into Afghanistan could have been provided from Peshawar and Quetta. This would have opened up space for a flourishing subcontracting sector in addition to transportation, hotels, restaurants, investment advisory firms, advertising agencies, representative offices, translators etc in our border cities.

All that may still be on the table but needs to be preceded by a top to bottom rethink of our objectives. What will it take to get us there? In one word: goodwill. It will mean that we should be able to do business with whatever government is in power in Afghanistan. You do not build goodwill by unleashing brigands or by taking sides in other people's internal conflicts. You build it by bringing them good things, widening their choices, by solving their problems and improving their lives. Trucks to Central Asia and pipelines from Turkmenistan will naturally follow not precede this outcome. But above all the new strategy objective must be to restore regional peace and help create a shared prosperity in which all sides be given a stake.

FROM GWADAR TO KASHGAR

July 2013

TWO and a half hours flying time from Islamabad lies Urumqi, capital of China's Xinjiang Uighur autonomous region. A further 320 kilometres beyond Urumqi's airport is the Eurasian continental pole of inaccessibility, the world's most landlocked spot.

From that vantage point the shoreline of Gwadar must appear as does land to a ship in mid-voyage through a great ocean.

And while a Gwadar to Kashgar corridor may not pretend to be the most viable route to China's eastern seaboard, where most of the population lives, Xinjiang itself is a sprawling landmass, home to 22 million people, and a $104 billion economy. It is a rich oil-producing region whose growth rate in the recent decade has outstripped the rest of China but the benefits of this growth have been lopsided. It still lags behind the rest of the country and the government in Beijing is keen to bring development to the region and also address the Uighur unrest.

One such significant initiative is the Urumqi Economic and Technological Development Zone that has attracted sizeable Chinese and foreign investment in projects that include manufacturing of wind power turbines, iron and steel, oil and gas drilling equipment as well as food and beverage and consumer products manufacturing.

Xinjiang region is adjacent to the Central Asian countries with which China has become the largest trading partner, ahead of even Russia. A large part of this is overland trade. Accordingly, for the Trade Development Authority of Pakistan (TDAP) the Horgos Free Trade Zone on the Xinjiang-Kazakhstan border might be worth looking into. As the largest land port in Western China this can serve as a springboard for Pakistani goods into the Central Asian region. This would circumvent Afghanistan where perpetual war (and warlordism) has blocked our access to the Central Asian region.

Meanwhile TDAP's counterpart, the Xinjiang region's bureau responsible for export and trade promotion, is making efforts to attract industry that can produce goods for Central Asia's future requirements for chemicals, farm products, capital goods, pharmaceuticals and renewable energy equipment.

Similarly, it plans to develop Kashgar, bordering our Gilgit-Baltistan into a regional logistics centre. Apart from cheap land, the planned fiscal incentives include tax exemptions, subsidised electricity and transport and low interest loans. Ultimately the Chinese vision is to bring Kashgar and Horgos at par with coastal boomtowns like Shenzhen and Xiamen.

Of course, the Chinese endeavour is to stimulate the production of goods in this region and then to get these goods out via land routes to neighbouring countries and via Gwadar to West bound destinations — towards Africa and Europe. Apart from finished goods this would also spur a regional trade in raw materials and intermediate goods and once again TDAP may be able to probe deeper into the potential emerging opportunities for Pakistani industrial produce here.

If one is to benefit from these developments then one has to go further afield than becoming a conduit to other people's cargo. Just naming a 2,000km stretch of road an 'economic corridor' does not make it one. In any event the term has become a deflated buzzword after the 'national trade corridor' of the Musharraf government which could not come to life.

Let's also not forget that for 12 years, Pakistan was a conduit for Nato containers with little economic benefit accruing from that activity, other than transit fee. For example, even bottled water supplies for the troops of the International Security Assistance Force were procured from Dubai.

We have to look beyond exporting our traditional finished goods, and towards integrating Pakistani manufacturing enterprises with regional production networks. In the heyday of the US automobile industry for example, General Motors would outsource the manufacture of many parts to vendors in Canada even if the final assembly was done in Detroit.

With some deeper probing, our Ministry of Industries and affiliated agencies such as the Small and Medium Enterprise Development Authority may be able to identify areas in agro processing, farm implements and textile and leather processing for instance where our value chains can be integrated with Chinese production networks in the Xinjiang region.

If on the other side, the same can be done with South Asian regional trade, then Pakistan emerges as the biggest beneficiary from the network effect that gets created.

There have been concerns in Pakistan about the Iranian port of Chahbahar, located on the same shoreline 70km from Gwadar and that

India will use it to access Afghanistan and Central Asia. While I am unable to digress and address the India-in-Afghanistan paranoia, I do not view the two ports as a zero-sum game. On the contrary I would suggest connecting both these ports with a 70km rail line so they could become alternate nodes in the same transport system.

Gwadar and Chahbahar though adjacent, point in different directions — one is oriented northeastwards towards China and eastern Afghanistan while the other is oriented towards western Afghanistan and the Caspian region.

The proposed interlinking would allow each country to access the other. In addition, there are economies of scale and complementarities from which both benefit. One of these could be Iran locating petrochemical facilities between the two ports. One has to look no further than the United Arab Emirates and find a number of seaports (and airports) close to each other and the entire region prospering as a highly efficient logistics and transport hub.

For its part, Pakistan must do its bit to allay Chinese concerns with opening the border and implications for the Uighurs' religiously-inspired militant separatist movement. In recent years, Pakistani sectarian groups have made inroads into the Gilgit-Baltistan region. These have to be put out of business and the area has to be cleansed because Pakistan's jihadis providing any stimulus or sanctuary to the Uighurs could become a show stopper.

REGIONAL CONNECTIVITY

February 2014

It is easy to be wise after the event. And one such wisdom has it that our blocking India's commercial access to Iran and Afghanistan was bad strategy. We have lost out on benefits that would have come from improved commercial and political ties among the regional states.

Decades of shunning economic interaction with a large next door neighbour, while linking everything to the dispute over Kashmir was also bad policy. India's economic growth rate in recent years has galloped and we found ourselves fenced out from an economy with which all other trading nations were lining up to do business with.

Similarly, trying to cultivate proxies in Afghanistan has not paid any dividends. That adventure has gone horribly wrong.

These inelegant strategies resulted from a strategy formulation process that, as one of its flaws, did not take economics into account.

The IPI gas pipeline was one initiative that would have given the regional countries a stake in the other's peace and stability while easing the energy constraint to economic growth. However, while that could not progress as a result of exogenous factors beyond our control, the others are clearly a result of our own bad choices.

In any event, the net result has been regional isolation. In a world where countries now trade mostly within their regions, we barely have any economic interaction in ours except for the Afghan transit trade.

The gradual opening up with India is a breath of fresh air. It has the potential to become a growth driver for Pakistan's economy.

Another key strategy piece to advance regional trade is the Gwadar port.

However, six years since its inauguration this port has still not earned its first million dollars. In fact Gwadar's true calling is to become the region's break-bulk hub. Presently, this business goes to ports and associated economic free zones in the United Arab Emirates. But Gwadar trumps these ports because its hinterland extends much deeper — into Central Asia. Why hasn't the government been able to attract break bulk operators to Gwadar? A business plan to make this happen should be an utmost urgency.

Further down, on the same shoreline is Iran's Chahbahar port. Blocked of overland access, India, Iran and Afghanistan reached a trilateral understanding in 2003 agreeing to develop a north-south corridor that would link Chahbabar with Afghanistan. India helped upgrade the port and in 2005, built the Afghanistan segment of the highway linking to the Afghanistan ring road. This meant that all major cities of Afghanistan could now connect with Chahbahar (in addition to Bandar Abbas).

The development fuelled Pakistan's paranoia of 'encirclement'. When construction crews working on the site came under relentless attacks from Taliban insurgents and a number of Indian engineers and Afghan workers were killed, the stakes went up. Shortly afterwards, Pakistan's Baloch regions experienced unrest with insurgents specially targeting energy infrastructure. The mutual mistrust deepened and the antagonism widened to include Iran and Afghanistan as well.

In 2009 the highway — Route 606 as it is known — was inaugurated and today is open and busy during daytime though not totally safe, so vehicles have to travel in convoys and with armed escorts.

The 3000-km Afghanistan ring road itself is a giant carousel with exits that branch out to Iran (at Chahbahar and Herat), to Turkmenistan, Uzbekistan and Tajikistan and to Pakistan (taking you to the Khyber Pass, the next one to Miramshah and the third one to Quetta). The proposed Trans Afghanistan pipeline or Tapi is planned to transport gas and its 1200 km journey from Daulatabad to Quetta will follow the alignment along the ring road.

A common regional vision needs to be developed within a regional matrix. It needs to serve the interests of the people that inhabit this region. All the regional countries stand to reap a substantial peace dividend if they can lower mistrust and mutual suspicions.

This will immediately reduce the levels of conflict and we will see trade, traffic and energy flow across national borders. Major initiatives can include extending land access, opening borders, building logistic infrastructure, and entering currency swap and free trade agreements.

Pakistan can gain substantially by connecting the Gwadar port to the Afghanistan ring road and get the port operating at capacity. It would also stand to gain from allowing overland access to the regional countries. A virtuous spiral of peace, economic activity and prosperity can be created that will heal wounds that have been festering for decades. And in this Pakistan has the most to gain.

RUSSIA'S OVERTURES

December 2014

THE endgame in Afghanistan appears to be trending towards a happy ending and Pak-Afghan-US relational harmony has never been better. At the same time we have seen an anxious Russia reach out to Pakistan in ways unprecedented.

How can we interpret the recent visit of the Russian Defence Minister, Sergei Shoigu and the sudden warming up in military ties?

Last month Shoigu led a 41-member delegation to Islamabad, at a time when the Pakistani army chief was himself visiting Washington. A defence cooperation agreement was also signed. A broader view of events seems to suggest that the Russians' visit was not about supplying 20 helicopters nor indeed about discussing the post US withdrawal situation in Afghanistan. It was about more immediate Russian concerns.

A week earlier Vladimir Putin had been at the G20 summit in Brisbane. Here he had been confronted and rebuked by Western leaders over actions in Ukraine. The strongest one had come from the Canadian Prime Minister Stephen Harper telling Putin: "I guess I'll shake your hand but I have only one thing to say to you, you need to get out of Ukraine."

On its part Russia feels boxed in by three factors. One is its sense of 'Western intrusion' into the former Soviet territories; the Baltic states are now snugly in Nato's embrace as also are two former Warsaw Pact countries. From Moscow's perspective its 'strategic depth' is rapidly shrinking, which may have prompted desperate actions in Crimea.

Secondly, the pivot of world power is also shifting from Europe (which the USSR as a land power once dominated) to Asia — with a locus in the South China Sea. And while Russia is striving for an important Asian role to maintain great power status it is limited by access to the southern Eurasian rimland that stretches from the Gulf of Aden to the Taiwan straits. Unlike the US it does not have a navy that can project power over such a vast distance.

The third factor is the collapse of oil prices which has struck a deathly blow to the Russian economy and currency. Together the three have made for a perfect storm.

China — rattled by pro-democracy protests in Hong Kong — had to face similar admonitions from Obama at the G20 summit. These were over its naval posturing against other states around the South China Sea as well as accusations of manipulating its currency which, the US believes, slows down its own economic recovery.

Immediately after the G20 summit Shoigu arrived in Beijing. Russia and China are keen to keep the US out of Asia and the Pacific and have evolved common interests directed against the US and its Nato allies. China for instance is dependent on Russia's aerospace technology which has developed high-speed and long-range aircraft needed to patrol Russia's vast airspace that spans 11 time zones. China, which lacks aircraft carriers, could make use of latest generation aircraft because they can operate from land bases, to protect its territorial claims in the South China Sea.

Yet, even as it has sold weapons to China, Russia has hedged against China militarily by arming India and Vietnam with even more sophisticated weapons, intended for use against China. Now, a major shift may be in the making, with China urging Russia to resolve this paradox. At any rate, India has recently been turning to the US for its arms requirements. Strategically, it would make sense for China to form a common front with Russia to counter Western naval presence in the Indian Ocean and the Western Pacific. Russia's news agency Tass quoted Shoigu in Beijing as saying that "strengthening and expanding ties with China remains Russia's overriding priority".

Two days after leaving Beijing, Shoigu and his delegation arrived in Islamabad. The visit was only announced a day before his arrival. It is likely that the Chinese may have helped facilitate the visit. Ideally Russia would like its warships to be able to draw logistic support from Pakistani ports. Russian warships have visited Karachi this year, something not seen in recent decades.

So where are we to go with all this? Russia is looking to sell arms. For Pakistan, new-generation Russian aircraft and submarines would be attractive offerings, if money can be found. Warships of friendly navies drawing logistic support at our ports during peacetime may also not be problematic.

Nevertheless, a major foreign policy shift — from our traditional orientation towards the West and Saudi Arabia — is neither possible nor desirable any time soon. While Russia can have ambitions of great power status, the Cold War is long over and in the globalised world of today it is economic interests rather than military rivalries that ought to shape our foreign policy.

RISE GWADAR

March 2015

THE opening of the Suez Canal in 1869 provided the British with a much shorter route to access their colonial possessions in India. With that, the importance of Aden as a transit and refuelling stop multiplied — sitting as it does, at the point where the Red Sea enters the Indian Ocean. The British made Aden part of its Indian holdings and by 1937 had turned it into a full-fledged crown colony. With that, Aden became one of the most important ship bunkering, trans-shipment and duty free ports in the world.

By 1967 decolonisation had almost run its course. Arab nationalism also peaked. When a local rebellion and uprising in Yemen forced the British to evacuate their naval base and ultimately get out of Aden, it was clear that its age of maritime pre-eminence was over.

Even before the oil riches had started to arrive in his little emirate, Dubai's Sheikh Rashid Al Maktoum was envisioning Dubai as the alternative to Aden. As the British were evacuating from Aden, he began constructing a deep water harbour, one that could service the world's largest vessels. Six years later, in 1972, Dubai's Port Rashid opened. A few years later as the oil riches arrived, the world's largest man-made port was constructed at Jebel Ali, opening Dubai's second port in 1979.

That was followed in 1985 by the Jebel Ali Free zone, a veritable entrepôt; complete with a free zone, an industrial area and sprawling warehousing and logistic facilities. Dubai's rise followed. Driven by political vision, executed on a master plan and enabled by a corporate structure, DP World, Dubai transformed itself into one of the world's largest trading hubs that it is today.

Of course, Japan's economic ascendency, followed by the Asian 'Tiger' economies and after 1980, the Chinese economic miracle, only bourgeoned Dubai's fortunes as world trade also flourished. The key trade corridor now ran along the Southern Eurasian rimland, which starts in Aden and runs all the way to Hong Kong. Now sitting on this corridor, waits Gwadar.

Its military utility apart, from a commercial perspective Gwadar can claim three distinct advantages over Dubai and the other Gulf ports that have followed a similar template. It lies on the main route, without vessels needing to enter the Straits of Hormuz. It has a large hinterland, which includes Pakistan, Afghanistan and at some point in future, Central Asia. Third, it offers a direct conduit to western China, which could be many times more valuable in the event of a blockage in the Straits of Malacca, a critical bottleneck. Dubai on the other hand enjoys the huge advantage of incumbency.

Gwadar's game plan needs to be ambitious, grandiose even. But hoping for things to fall in place by themselves is not good business strategy. 'Build it and they will come' is a dangerous mind trap. Gwadar's success will depend on the quality of the commercial strategy it pursues.

The first key will be crafting Gwadar's business model. This will detail how to make it a viable destination. It will include a marketing plan and an associated traffic forecast explaining how it will be achieved. Why will they come? What will they gain from coming here as opposed to going to other competitive ports in the region? Why would they switch from their traditional preference? The best consultants in the world cannot build your business models. That is a job the government's own 'Team Gwadar' must do.

The second key to success will be to build the critical mass of vessel traffic and cargo handling volumes needed for the port operator to break even. Gwadar port's business plan must achieve break even quickly. The port will drive the whole port city ecosystem, but only after it commercially takes off. The hard truth is that either it will achieve early commercial success or it will languish forever; like the railways where you have the infrastructure and even ready traffic but can't seem to make it work.

As I see it now, critical missing pieces include rail and pipeline connectivity, a processing zone, a cargo break-bulk area as well as a coherent investment attraction strategy that would lure break-bulk operators from neighbouring ports to relocate to Gwadar.

As it proceeds to operationalise the port the government must think about the answers to questions like who will use Gwadar. For instance, why will a container destined for Afghanistan or China opt to land in Gwadar as opposed to say Karachi or the neighbouring Iranian port of Chah Bahar? The time to play in the sand is over. It is time to start talking specifics. And that means talking business.

A CHINESE TEMPLATE

April 2015

TWO years ago, President Xi Jinping had first proposed the "One Belt, One Road", essentially a breakout economic vision for China. In an editorial this month, Hong Kong's South China Morning Post has described it as the most significant and far-reaching project the nation has ever put forward.

It seeks to expand the Chinese economy by first creating mega project construction opportunities for Chinese firms and then by spreading out markets for its manufactured goods. The plan is to accelerate growth in China's western regions and then integrate China's markets with Eurasia, the Middle East and Africa. Its one component, the Silk Road Economic Belt would connect Western China to Central Asia and Europe overland, while the other, the 21st-Century Maritime Silk Road would substantiate the link between Chinese seaports and the Middle East, Africa and the Mediterranean.

The Chinese then developed a blueprint to translate this vision into an action plan.

Days before President Xi's arrival in Pakistan the striking blueprint was revealed. "The Belt and Road run through the continents of Asia, Europe and Africa, connecting the vibrant East Asia economic circle at one end and the developed European economic circle at the other, and encompassing countries with huge potential for economic development." The editorial succinctly captured its essence: "Chinese companies [helping] to build the roads, railway lines, ports and power grids that are sorely needed in many parts of Asia, Africa and the Middle East. That, in turn, will involve loans and swap deals aimed at making the yuan a global currency." Long term it aims for "financial integration with the 65 Belt and Road countries across three continents". A Silk Road Fund and an Asian Infrastructure Investment Bank have been established to help finance these mega project initiatives.

That China has chosen to begin the implementation of this big bang template with Pakistan, one of its closest allies, is not surprising. It is being described as a significant opening move on the 'Belt and Road initiative' chessboard. The China Pakistan Economic Corridor (CPEC) is in fact a trunk passageway connecting the Silk Road Economic Belt in the north with the 21st-Century Maritime Silk Road in the south.

Additionally, branches from this trunk are also expected to connect Afghanistan, India and Iran with the Chinese 'Belt and Road' system. The blueprint document urges that "on the basis of respecting each other's sovereignty and security concerns, countries along the Belt and Road should improve the connectivity of their infrastructure ... and form an infrastructure network connecting all sub-regions in Asia, and between Asia, Europe and Africa step by step".

One can expect to see China urging Pakistan, India, Afghanistan and Iran to interconnect their road, grid and pipeline infrastructures with the CPEC trunk. The possible network effects this would create could conceivably be an even bigger economic bonanza for the region than the CPEC itself as the blueprint document contemplates removal of "investment and trade barriers for the creation of a sound business environment within the region and in all related countries". The Iran-Pakistan-India pipeline could be just one small example of this.

Explaining the modalities for execution, the document states that "China will work with countries along the Belt and Road to steadily advance demonstration projects, jointly identify programmes that ... are agreed upon by parties and ready for implementation, so as to ensure early harvest".

That for now most of the money has been allocated to coal-fired power plants reflects China's assessment of Pakistan's growth bottleneck — shortage of affordable energy. It is also where Chinese companies could provide the quickest assistance with financing options. Most of the rest of the money is to ease Pakistan's transport and logistics bottlenecks for regional connectivity.

Still other components include integrating industrial chains, clusters and parks so regional countries can build on their comparative advantage and entire industrial sectors can develop in concert. The document contemplates other forms of collaboration such as policy coordination and removal of non-tariff barriers among the countries. Most importantly, the Chinese cannot afford for the CPEC to flounder because most of the future success of the Belt and Road initiative may be predicated on its successful demonstration.

People have asked me what the catch is. Frankly, on combing the document I could not find one except to say that China may be projecting its soft (economic) power. On the other hand, there are two likely hazards on our side. One is the route controversy and the need is to urgently build political consensus and transparency. The other is bureaucratic incapacity and lethargy to execute the Pakistani side of the bargain. Islamabad needs to address both of these on a war footing.

CPEC FAULTERING?

November 2015

I hope I am wrong on this one. But early signs indicate that the Pakistani side has already started faltering on the China Pakistan Economic Corridor. This has happened within six months after its announcement with much fanfare during the visit of Chinese President Xi Jinping.

Last week the parliamentary committee was given a 'status update' by the executing ministries. The 'briefing' consisted of a presentation on the FWO's (Frontier Works Organisation) progress on the Western route, another on the Suki Kinari power project and standard presentations on coal deposits that are available in Khyber Pakhtunkhwa and Balochistan and about which we have known about for a long time. Another one was on opportunities in the agriculture sector.

So the Western route is being built and hopefully will be completed by the end of 2016. Trucks laden with shipping containers will be able to ply up and down. But does the government have any estimate or study that can quantify the economic benefits that will accrue from this? NATO containers also plied our roads for over a decade but what then? Sure there will be ribbon development effects and we'll see refueling stations, rest areas and tea shops crop up alongside the new route. Hinterland access would also be improved as branches are developed from the trunk. But to be sure, the CPEC is a north-south trunk that meets the Chinese objective of accessing markets for its manufactured goods. Do we have any ideas, apart from the usual platitudes, on leveraging it to create substantial economic benefits?

To be fair, China has suggested for Pakistan to establish industrial parks and special economic zones where raw materials and other factors of production are available. Industrial parks can be considered for sectors such as steel, cement, automobiles, construction materials, gems and stones, household appliances, agricultural implements, textiles and garments. With some savvy business structuring, it may even be possible to relocate certain low technology industries from China. For several weeks, the Federal and provincial governments went through the usual standard motions, and identified sites for 29 industrial parks and 21 special economic zones.

But the government remained clueless on how these estates will be made attractive for investors. Who will invest here, what will they make and who will they sell to? What ails our competitiveness in most productive industrial sectors? Indeed why so many existing industrial estates in the country remain underutilized.

Instead of any deep thinking on the matter the government was last mulling exemptions from duties and taxes on all imported machinery and a 20 year income tax holiday for new manufacturing plants. That is, until somebody mentioned the elephant in the room. How do we run industrial estates without electricity? And that was that. Now even this half-baked plan has been put off because there is not enough electricity. Clearly the government is out of ideas here. If it had its piece together, the electricity bit was easy to solve. Let the estate developers & operators bring in rental power plants. Any excess could be fed to the grid and any shortfall drawn from it. They would need fuel to be delivered to their locations. And the fastest stop gap solution would be furnace oil. At present low world oil prices this may just be viable. Until we can get our power plants up and running that is.

Incidentally most issues appear to revolve around the power sector. To the earlier problem of circular debt and delayed payments has now been added a decrepit grid that cannot evacuate and transmit power in the required quantities. And project sponsors in the power sector complain that there is no "one window" as promised, instead they have to chase around AEDB, NEPRA, NTDC and other power sector agencies separately to get their files and paperwork processed; the work at each window is dependent on the other and the agencies do not talk to each other to resolve problems.

On to Gwadar port where 1,000 hectares have been assigned to the port operator, China Overseas Port Holding Company to develop a duty free zone and industrial area adjacent to the port. In my background discussions with the company, it was not clear to them yet what kind of business opportunities would be pursued at the zone, whether the investors would predominantly come from China or from the local market. There does not appear to be a traffic forecast with underlying assumptions indicating how many and what type of ships will arrive in 2018, 2019 and 2020? The port operator appeared to be struggling with these questions. The government needs to step up and ask them what is it that we can do to help you get this port up and running. The government needs to allocate more imagination and will here.

... ...

ENERGY

Despite being endowed with large indigenous energy reserves and capacity to tap these resources, Pakistan has not been able to unlock this potential. Following the global financial crisis of 2008, and the sharp rise in world energy prices, this issue came to a fore. This section explores certain key themes in Pakistan's struggles with energy issues that were to dogit over the coming decade.

PAKISTAN'S ENERGY FUTURE

August 2009

The rental power plants are, at best, a quick and dirty fix. A quicker and cleaner one might have been if last winter the turbine blades in the government's own generation plants had been replaced with modern, aerodynamic designs.

That action alone would have added a few percentage points in efficiency to plants like Guddu, Shahdara and Kotri and to KESC's at Bin Qasim.

Today the result would have been a few hundred extra megawatts in capacity — gained without burning a single gallon of furnace oil — and higher approval ratings for the PPP government. Arguably the cost could have been financed through raising debt against future receivables from the additional output and through a carbon credits programme as the increased efficiency would reduce greenhouse gas emissions.

The Government of Pakistan is now expected to be writing a plan on how it proposes to overcome the power shortage. Meanwhile, a US team arranged by the Obama administration's point man in Pakistan, Richard Holbrooke, is also presently in Pakistan to make its own assessments. If this arrangement works well, the Holbrooke team will also provide inputs into the GoP's plan, then carry out a final review and make recommendations. If the GoP accepts those recommendations, the US administration will use its influence to get this plan funded.

In writing this plan, a good starting point for the government would be to define plan objectives that have measurable benchmarks. For instance, the planners may want to lay down 'promotion of socio-economic development (and justice)' and 'the sharpening of Pakistan's competitive advantage in agriculture and certain industrial sectors' as the energy plan's objectives. Lowering the cost of energy is akin to raising GDP per capita as it leaves more purchasing power in the hands of households. It also drives down the cost of doing businesses.

Other objectives could include energy security, the development of indigenous resources and saving of foreign exchange. Whilst Pakistan's energy mix is skewed towards oil and natural gas, still, and rather remarkably, three quarters of energy needs are met by domestic resources. Indigenous oil and gas reserves, however, are depleting faster than new discoveries are being made. Accordingly, this ratio is fast falling. As another objective, the plan could aim to redress or reverse this trend.

The 14-year delay in developing the Thar coal reserves has brought home two lessons. One, fuel and electricity need to be dealt with in an integrated way. Two, Islamabad must not play tug-of-war with the provinces.

The power sector can be best optimised if the brief is expanded to include transport fuels, renewable energy, conservation initiatives and the carbon trading mechanism. At present, these are scattered across the ministries of petroleum, communications, agriculture and environment, while others are with the Planning Commission and still others with the provincial (in some cases even city) governments.

If upgrading four turbines can take so long one can imagine the mental exhaustion when these additional bureaucracies get involved. Probably as a way to avoid getting bogged down in management frustrations, Pakistan's energy planners and Richard Holbrooke's team of experts may be tempted to limit the plan only to the power sector.

This would be suboptimal. It would pose two risks one, that this narrow approach may defy an optimal solution, and two, that inefficiencies and costs may instead be shifted or imposed elsewhere. To preclude these, the planners need to be given a larger sandbox in which to play. The energy sector needs to be dealt with in an integrated way.

Natural gas is an exhaustible resource. Coal — given the size of Thar's reserve — is not. For this reason it is central to Pakistan's energy solution. Half of the world's electricity is generated from coal. The Thar coal seam lies 130-250m under the desert and for the most part, sandwiched between water tables above and below the coal seam. This poses a mining challenge.

The coal is lignite and of low rank. It has a tendency to spontaneously combust when brought out to the open. This poses storage, transport and a general logistic challenge. Also because it has high sulphur content it emits large quantities of sulphur dioxide when burnt. This poses conversion challenges.

Together these challenges limit the options. Not long ago coal was a dirty fuel. Today, there are clean technologies; a popular one is underground gasification in which the coal never sees the sky. Instead, compressed air is piped down into the coal seam in a way to change its molecular structure and turn it into gas which is then recovered as it gushes out from beneath the surface. The process involves costs but saves on mining, handling, transportation and cleaning the coal.

The resulting gas — syngas — can be used as a fuel in its own right or further converted to natural gas. It can be used for power generation, as transportation fuel and for the production of fertilisers and chemicals. The technology is nothing new. However, the process is capital-intensive and requires know-how. This is where Holbrooke's team and Pakistan's allies are needed most.

Coal gasification also offers a halfway house where environmentalists and 'developmentalists' coming as they do from opposite directions, can meet and shake hands.

Pakistan's total energy requirement works out to a little over 100m tons of coal equivalent (mtce) each year. In addition another 50 mtce is provided by burning firewood, dung and crop residues in the rural sector. This uncharted opportunity for biofuels and natural fertilisers is at present outside the mandate of the planners.

Farm waste augmented by jatropha grown on marginal lands can be converted to biofuels, and their residues to organic fertilisers. These together with local wind and solar energy solutions can meet the entire energy requirement of the rural sector. Such programmes have shown to raise rural incomes and alleviate poverty in Latin America and sub-Saharan Africa and must be included in the terms of reference for this plan.

The Kalabagh experience taught us that power cannot be dealt with separately from the water issue. The real world often requires us to handle more complex things than changing a light bulb; even if to an energy saver, or, for that matter, changing four-turbine blades. But first, let's get the big picture right.

A REFRESHING BREEZE

February 2013

FOLLOWING a splendid lunch of char-grilled pomfret and chili crabs I was lying — with our beach hut behind me — on the sand facing the shimmering ocean.

On one side the waterline gradually curves outwards to form the cape popularly known as the French Beach. Beyond that, out in the distance, stands the Karachi Nuclear Power Plant.

Kanupp was built by the Canadians and commissioned in 1972 as Pakistan's first nuclear reactor designed to add 137 megawatts of electricity to the grid. However, because Pakistan refused to sign the Nuclear Non-Proliferation Treaty unless India also signed it, the Canadians discontinued support and the plant has barely ever run at a fraction of its capacity. Now, the Kanupp that lay before me had completed its 40-year design life and was to be decommissioned.

After Kanupp, it took 23 years before a new type of fuel was used to generate electricity for the grid, when the Lakhra coal power plant in Sindh was fired up. Conceived in 1986 it was commissioned nine years later — in 1995.

Eleven difficult years later, in 2006 it came to a grinding halt. Whilst there were said to be some technical issues relating to corrosion problems in the pipes, the main showstoppers appeared to be management and legal difficulties.

Since the plant ran on local coal which is available in abundance from nearby mines, one cannot think of any insurmountable financial difficulties either. However, the project has not just languished but no other coal power plant has been built after 1995.

Coming from this perspective, the Jhimpir wind power projects that are starting to come on stream this year represent the first drops of rain after a 17-year drought. Jhimpir is in a good neighbourhood — 418 kilometres across a desert and a border in the Indian state of Rajasthan lies the Suzlon Group's 1,000MW Jaisalmer Wind Park, one of the largest wind farms in the world.

Based on satellite mapping of wind resources at a height of 50 metres above the ground, by the United States National Renewable Energy Laboratory, experts estimate the onshore potential of the Hyderabad-Gharo-Keti Bandar corridor at 50,000MW.

Estimates can vary on how much is exploitable. Experts talk about a 32 per cent "capacity factor" which basically takes into account the days the wind blows and the days it doesn't. Nevertheless, thousands of megawatts can be generated. In particular, the hills and ridges between Karachi and Hyderabad are the sweetest spots for wind energy production.

Behind FFC and Zorlu, the two projects that come on stream in early 2013, there are another 30 with a collective potential of 1,800MW in progress and at various stages of the pipeline. Some are looking for land, others are conducting feasibility studies, and a few are waiting for generation licences from the National Electric Power Regulatory Authority.

Clearly this flurry of business activity is the result of some good work done by the Alternative Energy Development Board and the Sindh government, proof that good policy formulation and attractive incentives can produce results, even in an adverse political and economic climate.

In Pakistan, some economic sectors have attracted saturation levels of investment. The leading ones are banking, telecos, TV channels and independent power plants. The IPPs would have attracted still greater investment had they not become plagued with circular debt. What was common across these sectors was the combination of a sound policy framework, transparency and an independent and strong regulator.

Wind-based power generation is just a sub-sector within the independent power production sector. The largest commercial impediment to investment in the power generation business in Pakistan today is the issue of circular debt and timely payments to IPPs. It may appear that wind-based IPPs are cushioned against this because late payments would not cause suspension of "fuel supply". There is the risk that these IPPs may therefore be relegated to the bottom of the pecking order. This would be bad vision and even worse governance.

These projects are motivated by commercial considerations, backed by financial institutions and funded by shareholders that have reposed their trust in the project sponsors. In turn the project sponsors have reposed their trust in the guarantees given by the Pakistan government.

Moral principals apart, the journey from Kanupp to Lakhra to Jhimpir has been a long one and a new form of fuel, harnessing of wind potential, now appears within reach. On the other side of the Rann of Kutch, the Indian state of Gujarat alone is producing 3,000MW from similar wind conditions. Further south, Tamil Nadu is doing 7,000MW.

There's no reason why Sindh cannot approach these numbers. Like a newborn child, the wind energy sector must be incubated against the circular debt trap and other forms of risk. Good business sense would tell us that further encouragement to this sector sends out positive vibes to other investors and keeps the pipeline flowing.

As the projects come on stream one by one, each dollar of power purchased from the wind IPPs would offset 93 cents from the burgeoning import of furnace oil. The $700 million received in December under the Coalition Support Fund was immediately used up to import furnace oil which has been fed into the system and will be gobbled up in transmission losses, nonpayment and theft.

Of course there's no running away from fixing the root causes of circular debt. Till that is done, payments to the wind IPPs must be kept current.

An entrepreneur would tell you that when you hit upon a formula that works, repeating it over and over again; replicating it many times is the key to creating wealth and value. In that sense we must see more and more wind projects being created through this process.

The government must also replicate successful policy and regulatory frameworks that have worked in the past and adapt these for other economic sectors.

OFFSHORE OIL AND GAS

February 2013

SOME time ago over a dinner in Rome an Italian friend had introduced me to Ennio Marcella, a marine scientist from Naples.

Ennio had a charming demeanour and with his sunburnt face and inquisitive eyes it was not difficult for me to visualise him lugging his fishing gear and adjusting scientific instruments on board his catamaran as it left the rugged Amalfi coast heading into a sun-drenched Mediterranean.

During our conversation he developed a keen interest not just in visiting Pakistan but bringing his boat too. It wasn't exactly a catamaran from what he explained because his exploration vessel was in fact fitted with sonar and acoustic equipment which could carry out seismic investigations to map and estimate resource potential deep below the ocean floor.

This data could then be turned into intellectual property and using various subscriber models, revenue could be generated.

Of course it takes a lot of money to run the vessel up and down an 1100-kilometre coastline and where the coastal water extends some 200 nautical miles (370km) into Pakistan's exclusive economic zone.

He told me he'd be happy if in the end a slice of the intellectual property could be given to him as his royalty. He was confident that the initiative would spur the development of Pakistan's offshore resources leading to possible discoveries of offshore oil and gas.

It was much later that I learnt that a clunky, old Russian vessel with primitive equipment while on a mapping expedition of the Arabian Sea in the 1960s had discovered the Bombay High. This single oilfield, located 160km offshore from Mumbai today produces 14 per cent of India's total requirement of crude oil.

The neighbouring Indian state of Gujarat has abundant oil and gas reserves, as has Sindh including underneath Badin, almost touching the ocean. With Gujarat having recently struck offshore gas, the prospect of a gas find offshore from Sindh is bright. The region is also close to refineries, pipelines, consumption centres around Karachi, power plants and planned LNG terminals.

And whilst Pakistan can boast an impressive success rate for new discovery — 30 per cent of all exploration wells that have been dug and have yielded oil or gas — very little offshore exploration has been done.

Even then the dozen or so wells that have been drilled have not yielded anything in commercial quantities. The seismic investigation data that Ennio was proposing to generate would not only spur offshore exploration activity but also potentially improve the success rate.

The problem with the royalty formula was that Ennio would not receive any form of remuneration for quite some time.

On the other hand he would need some cash flow to sustain operations for the months and years he would spend charting our territorial waters. To partly finance that he could access research grants from the European Union and for that a nod from the Pakistan government would greatly help. For the remainder he suggested that if he could be granted a fishing licence he could then bridge the remaining gap.

Now I am aware of the controversy that surrounds deep sea fishing and yet in Pakistan the production levels are well within sustainable yields. It is another matter that the sector is not properly regulated. When regulations are not properly enforced some of the practices of the foreign operators result in collateral damage to marine life.

He would get a head start if he could get his hands on any oceanographic information on fish zones and on ocean topography which refers to the highs and lows of the seabed inside Pakistani territorial waters.

Now usually governments, including ours, have legislation and methods to evaluate and process such — unsolicited — proposals received from educational, commercial or nonprofit entities.

So on returning to Pakistan I forwarded Ennio's suggestions to the Board of Investment that operates as a 'one window' facility and is supposed to process proposals on fast track. To give it the necessary clout it is kept under the prime minister's secretariat. On a lighter note, I have overheard investors scoff at this, terming it one more window.

I do not know what happened after that but let me conjecture — because it will offer a glimpse into the underlying reasons behind the investors' cynicism as well as the governmental paralysis and the inability of the Pakistani state to function at any level. And before we start pointing figures at the ruling coalition it is my contention that the following would have happened regardless of who the political masters may have been.

A file was opened and "parawise [sic] noting" begun, from one office to another, routed to the Ministry of Science and Technology, from there to the Ministry of Ports and Shipping, and yes, because the proposal includes deep sea fishing, that approval would need to come from the Ministry of Food, Agriculture and Livestock (MinFAL).

If its functions haven't been devolved already then MinFAL would have wanted to bring on board the two provincial governments (Sindh and Balochistan) with their own layers of bureaucracy.

Then of course the defence ministry would have to be consulted because 'strategic' offshore resources (even if presently nonexistent) are involved. The ministry of course would not decide without taking the Navy, the Coast Guards and the Maritime Security Agency into confidence and of course the intelligence agencies because high-tech equipment is involved.

And all this even before any commercial or legal evaluation has begun.

Round and round and round, there is nowhere for the buck to stop; where every government office is a post office and every official is either a gatekeeper or a postman.

Endless activity, reams of paper, meetings, committees, task forces but nothing moves on the ground, and that, dear reader, is the story of how Pakistan is run.

WILL LOADSHEDDING END?

April 2013

HOW long will we live with loadshedding? Will the next government be able to fix the problem during its term?

I have to admit I have not gone into the party manifestos in great detail. I have no doubt they all have well-meaning and lofty plans of increasing generation capacity, improving the fuel mix, improving distribution efficiencies and tackling the root causes of circular debt. No quarrel with that.

There is no shortage of plans collecting dust in the government archives as well. We all know what needs doing. The question is how do you get the plan funded? According to estimates, Pakistan will need $10 billion in capital spending to deal with the power crisis in the coming years and another double this amount to build large dams. Let's see where we can find the first $10bn.

Public funding is out of the question. The exchequer, already burdened with billions of dollars of circular debt, will not be able to absorb such large capital expenditures. The next possibility is to look at the multilateral financial institutions (MFIs) like the World Bank and the Asian Development Bank.

MFIs may finance technical and feasibility studies, they may even co-fund projects in hydropower and provide concessional loans to undertake grid improvement projects.

Similarly, the bilateral assistance agencies such as the USAID may offer project specific assistance for such things as capacity building of personnel and very specific efficiency improvement projects. From the money received under the Kerry Lugar act, for example, the turbines of some public-sector plants were upgraded to release a few hundred additional megawatts.

Still, it would be naïve to expect the international agencies to play more than a marginal role in financing Pakistan's energy plan.

Under the power sector reforms that began in 1997, the Water and

Power Development Authority (Wapda) was unbundled and vertically disintegrated into independent generation companies (Gencos); distribution companies (DISCOs) and a transmission company (NTDC). The National Electric Power Regulatory Authority was created as the industry regulator.

That process has remained stalled with the result that where the benefit of experience and central planning (under Wapda) has been lost, the intended gains from better market efficiencies have not been realised. What we have today is the worst of both worlds.

The incoming government will need to complete the transition to the industry regime of the future; that is based on competition, open access and market-based pricing. Like the imposition of value-added tax and agriculture income tax this will not come without a great deal of pain; a major reason why all governments since 1997 have been reluctant to complete the power-sector reforms.

Even if the incoming government is able to cut through all the bureaucratic red tape, the reforms will take a minimum of two painful years to complete. Immediately after that, Pakistan will be able to turn to the most plausible source of financing for its energy plan: private capital.

In a distressed world economy, investors seek watertight guarantees. Power plants commissioned under the 2002 power generation policy have, in recent years, faced frequent and prolonged shutdowns on account of fuel shortages — natural gas and furnace oil. When the existing plants are lying idle, seeking new investors is frustrating.

A key decision the incoming government will need to make is on the choice of fuels going forward. There is a moratorium on building new furnace oil and natural gas-fired power plants.

Unfortunately, coal has recently become a no-no with most of the international financial community (except China, but for coal transportation, railways would need to move first). Nuclear and hydropower are very long term. Alternate energy — wind and solar — are good options but cannot yet become mainstay.

One way to fast track investment would be to revive the 1994 power policy; specifically the clause relating to capacity payments; while the reforms are under way on a parallel track.

The stumbling block here would be the issue of furnishing larger sovereign guarantees. Pakistan's financial limits to provide any further guarantees are already overstretched.

To circumvent this, the new government may access the MFIs' programmes that extend sovereign and political risk cover to investors where governments in developing countries are unable to.

The challenge here is that even if done at full speed, the preparation of paperwork and processing time for an application is about 18 months. In addition, the MFIs often have their own set of conditions they want the government to sign.

But this process will remove political risk, and with reforms taking place on a parallel track, the new government will be able to start attracting investment for new projects. By this time it would be about two years into its term. Even if the plants are then built at record speed of three years — these would be commissioned after the five-year term of the incoming government has ended in 2018. And that, dear reader, is the answer to the title of this column.

The silver lining is that we can expect the thermal and small hydro projects that are already in the pipeline to start coming on-stream during the next five years — on the proviso that they're able to achieve financial close.

If the incoming government shows sufficient will to take the energy sector reforms forward, then that pipeline will deliver energy projects a lot faster. A great deal of that work has already been laid out for the next government. The will to push through the reform is what is now needed.

RESTORING POWER SUPPLIES

June 2013

TALK of efficient and inefficient power generation plants at this stage is largely a red herring. It detracts focus from the main issue. You cannot run a modern economy without electricity.

Expensive electricity or more expensive electricity is only a question of degree. Either one is better than no electricity.

True there is no quick fix, no magic wand, but there is the immediate term and beyond that is the short-term. Apart from rental power there is no immediate fix. Inefficient plants are still cheaper than rental power. Under the present circumstances firing up all boilers would be the best choice.

According to Ministry of Water and Power estimates, this would involve a running cost of Rs3.5 billion per day, mostly for fuel supplies. With all thermal plants running, plus the additional hydroelectric power that — with the dams beginning to release water — is being added to the grid each day, the load-shedding can be brought down to about four hours a day.

Meanwhile the Planning Commission tells us the other half of the story. Of the Rs3.5bn sought by the Ministry of Water and Power, recoveries from consumers will fetch only Rs2.5bn while Rs1bn would be "lost" every day.

Half of this would be in "tariff differential" — which is the difference between production cost and selling price — and the other half in line losses and outright pilferage. This is how a billion rupees get added to the mountain of circular debt each day.

A sharp increase in electricity rates is therefore unavoidable. The public must be informed that prices will have to go up before they can come down, that is if they can be brought down at all by means of a more favourable fuel mix.

Using a combination of tariff increases, better management of the utility companies and discriminate (as opposed to across the board) load-shedding, it is possible to minimise, if not eliminate, the Rs1bn daily losses. This can be achieved in the short term.

While referring to the power bureaucracy the caretaker minister for water and power was recently heard saying that he had not seen such corruption and incompetence in his whole life.

In other words, nothing short of a massive purge here would work and this would need to be coupled with bringing in a clean and efficient top management for all the generation companies, distribution companies and the National Transmission & Despatch Company.

That too would be an interim solution, pending privatisation. Another required feature of this new management is for it to be pro-privatisation, which will be their main brief.

Finally, if the brunt of load-shedding is made to fall on distribution zones with poor revenue recovery, then that measure can contain losses.

The suggested approach has three payoffs. One, elimination of the Rs1bn daily losses means a steady power supply which is also economically sustainable.

Two, the additional electricity brought into the system is the (presently scarce) factor of production that is most needed for economic revival.

Three, it frees the government's energy team from firefighting, to focus on the more fundamental issues of carrying out reform and enhancing generation capacity.

As the lights come back on we can begin to talk about plant efficiencies. The public-sector plants offer the greatest opportunity for efficiency enhancement. This is achieved by retrofitting them with more aerodynamic turbines and with combined cycle technology.

Because these initiatives aim to squeeze out more electricity from the same quantity of fuel, they offer a high return on investment and find willing financiers.

On the other hand, we are hearing a lot of talk of coal-power generation. As I've cautioned in my article on April 28 'Will load-shedding end?' this route has its challenges — not least among which is raising international financing given that coal is this century's villain in a world where climate change is a major worry.

In addition, building a coal supply chain requires extraordinary backhaul and logistic capabilities.

To put things in perspective, the daily coal requirement of a 500-megawatt power plant is around 4,000 tons.

If this is imported coal it equates to a train — a diesel locomotive pulling 30 wagons — leaving the seaport for the power plant every eight hours. If this is local coal it involves 150 large-sized dump trucks each day from mine mouth to plant, and a mining and engineering infrastructure in place that can steadily deliver coal in such quantities.

These are continuous logistical operations on a scale that is unprecedented in Pakistan. Getting to this stage may take a few years and the proposal is not something that can be seriously considered for the short-term.

Nevertheless, a short-term coal challenge for the government may be to rehabilitate the Lakhra coal-fired power plant for which local coal is available from nearby mines. Beyond that it can pick up the Karachi Electric Supply Company's coastal Bin Qasim plant as a candidate for coal conversion.

Another good starting point is to look at the projects in the pipelines of the Private Power and Infrastructure Board, the Water and Power Development Authority and the Alternative Energy Development Board.

From here it can identify the dozen or so thermal, hydro and wind power projects that are closest to fruition and where government intervention may be able to help bring some of the commissioning dates forward.

All these of course are stop-gap measures, which if not accompanied by energy-sector reforms will unravel quickly.

Another hard one to swallow is that there is a world market for energy prices, from which Pakistan cannot remain immune. Instead of resisting that reality, the sooner we come to terms with it, the sooner we'll be able to find a way out of our energy troubles.

PAYING IT OFF

June 2013

SO we are told that the government plans to retire the circular debt and restore power supplies.

Under the present circumstances, it is hard to imagine a better policy stimulus that will spur supply side growth. One hoped, however, that the money would be raised more prudently, on the fiscal side; either through austerity measures or by collecting taxes owed by those who don't file returns.

Perhaps because these are difficult policy choices, the government, preferring the path of least resistance, has looked to the monetary side. From here it intends to raise circa Rs500 billion through a treasury bill auction. In layman terms, this is known as printing money.

The last time such a clean slate solution was attempted was in 2009, when most of the Rs200bn debt was moved off Pepco's (Pakistan Electric Power Company) balance sheet and on to a newly created power holding company.

This company in turn repackaged the debt and sold it as term finance certificates. Back at that time, this financial wizardry was also mooted to be a "one off" affair. This is a crude form of an asset class known in the world of finance as derivatives.

Monetary measures on this scale are not without their macroeconomic effects and inflationary impact. Arguably this money will be incremental to the 'business as usual' deficit financing that our governments consider routine.

Unlike fiscal measures which can be targeted, these have an inflationary impact which falls on the poorer segments of society. It would also appear to leave less money on the table for other economic stimuli, such as recapitalising the state-owned enterprises, if the government is planning to turn them around.

Others may argue that the Rs500bn T-bill auction would also reduce liquidity for the private sector, which is clamouring for credit at low interest rates. To put things in perspective, in 2009 the total outstanding credit to the textile sector alone was Rs535bn. As electricity supplies resume, so will the appetite of this industry — which generates over half of our total exports — for working capital expand.

The other important consideration is to ensure that the circular debt does not accumulate all over again. A sharp increase in electricity prices alone is not enough. The previous government also doubled prices during its tenure. Tough reforms across the energy sector are needed.

Which brings us to the essential question; is the government up to taking some tough policy decisions early in its tenure? Or, as with the T-bill, would it choose some easy, circumventing path?

Even after taking all the tough and unpopular policy decisions, the structural anomalies that produce the circular debt will take time to fix. During this time the circular debt will, in all probability, build up again. One more round of retirement may be necessary. The size of that pile will depend on how quickly the government is able to carry through its reform process and bring the power supplies to economically sustainable levels.

In all this there is a silver lining. If a monetary expansion on the one side is accompanied by an increase in aggregate supply on the other, then arguably the two should cancel each other out and the inflationary impact would be neutral.

If this is what the government's economic planners are hoping to achieve then it is a risky but nevertheless a justifiable executive decision. The risk is that the money is being printed first and after that if output doesn't expand, then we're left to deal with the inflationary effects.

But beyond that, let's look at circular debt more closely. At the bottom of the cascade, it ends up as money payable to four companies, three of which are producers of primary energy in Pakistan, the Oil & Gas Development Company, Pakistan Petroleum Ltd and Mari Petroleum, while the fourth, Pakistan State Oil, is the country's main importer of primary energy.

All trains terminate here. Excepting Wapda's hydropower units, the other players in the energy chain, the refineries, the public-sector generation companies, the gas utility companies, the independent power producers, the distribution companies et al are intermediary stations leading up to the top of the cascade where sits the consumer. What may not be so obvious is that the money — the Rs500bn — is also there. It is not lost. It is available in the form of unpaid electricity bills, and most of these pertain to federal, provincial and local government entities.

Others pertain to commercial entities that invariably have disputes with their power utilities over the amount. In addition part of the Rs500bn may well be normal payables and receivables which make up for the working capital of the energy companies. Financial prudence would require the government to retire the Rs500bn T-bill as the revenue from these unpaid bills materialises.

Provision of electricity will fuel aggregate supply. But beyond that there will be other benefits. As the liquidity crunch ends and choke points are removed, the biggest beneficiaries will be the oil and gas sector, in anticipation of which the Karachi Stock Exchange has enjoyed an unprecedented rally in recent weeks.

During its tenure the previous government must have poured over Rs1.5 trillion into the power sector. Each summer Punjab would erupt in violent protests, the prime minister would call for an energy conference. It was, however, unable to follow up with the (politically unpopular) reforms. That is where all eyes will be in the coming weeks.

THE ENERGY CHALLENGE

May 2014

IT was a freezing winter night in 2010 and I had just checked into the government rest house at the Lal Sohanra national park when the lights had gone out. The caretaker at the premises had lit a bonfire in the sprawling backyard which extended on one side to the edge of a lake.

"This is Nawaz Sharif's favourite spot sahib, right where you are sitting. Been here several times, and we would chat late into the night sometimes" he told me as we warmed our hands in the bonfire heat. "The younger one is more reserved ... he's a grouch. But the elder one's very relaxed. Oh, and he loves to listen to the flute" he went on to disclose.

Recently, Prime Minister Nawaz Sharif returned here to inaugurate the Quaid-i-Azam solar park. Situated on the edge of the Cholistan desert near Bahawalpur, the region which is famous for its peacock, gazelle and black buck is now set to become the world's largest solar park. Investment commitments totalling nearly 1,000 megawatts have already been received from local and Chinese business groups.

Energy requirement and economic growth are strongly correlated. Pakistan's per capita energy demand is one fifth of the world average. Electric power is a factor of production presently in short supply. And it is holding back economic growth.

The present peak electricity demand is estimated at 25,000MW while studies indicate that to cater to the projected electricity demand, an additional 100,000MW of capacity would need to be installed over the medium term.

One limitation of renewable energy is its fluctuating availability. Solar power is only available during daytime, wind power when there is breeze and hydropower is dependent on the ebb and flow of the water. This keeps renewable energy from becoming the mainstay in the overall energy mix. For this reason the base load in most grid systems is carried by thermal (and nuclear) power stations which can provide a steady supply all day and all year.

One would imagine urban solid waste to be a steadier source of fuel. But scavenging at various stages of the waste management process and inelegant waste disposal and handling mechanisms make it hard to work with. The end result is high cost-per-ton of fuel.

Similarly biomass generated in the agriculture and livestock sector fulfils about a third of Pakistan's total primary energy requirement. This, like so much else in this country, takes place in the non-commercial sector and remains undocumented. Nevertheless, projects can be conceived and commercialised where crop residues and animal dung is purchased from the farmers for conversion to higher forms of energy while simultaneously creating markets for this energy.

A successful commercial model will be one that can extract more energy from the same quantity of fuel, creating enough value to recompense farmers for the forgone fuel; with which they can buy their energy requirements from the market and still have money left over.

Such a model will bring parts of the rural subsistence economy into the commercial, documented economy. This way, much of the future growth can be based on indigenous fuel.

Contrary to what many believe, all renewable energy is not cheap. The present wind and solar power tariffs are close to what is being paid to oil-based Independent Power Producers and twice as high as the 8.5 US cents that was offered to private hydropower producer, Laraib Energy, a couple of years ago.

Dams at Bunji, Diamer-Bhasha, Dasu and Kalabagh (if consensus can be built) can potentially contribute 20pc of the projected requirement of 100,000MW. Other smaller dams, biomass, wind and solar potential should be tapped to the maximum extent possible. The base load will, however, need to be carried by thermal (including coal) and nuclear.

Assuming a benchmark price of $1.3 million per installed megawatt, the country would need an investment of $130 billion in the next 15 to 20 years. To put this figure in perspective, the total foreign direct investment, or FDI, in Pakistan in the last 50 years in all business sectors is in the region of $20bn.

However, lately, perhaps because of our failure to carry through reforms in the power sector, sensing a lack of seriousness to fix the structural issues, players like Xenel, National Power and AES have left Pakistan after selling off their stakes.

The key to overcoming the energy challenge, then, lies in the governance of the energy sector.

RESPONSIBLY PLEASE

September 2014

THAT reservations over the Pak-China bilateral coal power projects were raised in rabble-rousing forums instead of the sober atmosphere of a parliamentary committee is unfortunate. Whatever the merits of the objections to the proposed deals, they ought to have been raised in a more responsible manner. Further damage can be averted if we clear the air, unbundle some of the issues and see how these project opportunities have evolved.

Last summer the incoming PML-N government released the National Power Policy 2013. As one of the policy objectives, the weighted average cost of producing electricity was to be brought down. To do this the policy proposed to characteristically change the energy mix — from gas, which is a depleting resource, and furnace oil, which is an expensive fuel, to coal.

Over the longer term, the policy proposed to tap the hydropower potential of the Indus Basin cascade at sites like Thakot, Patan and Dasu and subsequently at Bunji and Diamer-Basha. Coal, it was felt was not just economical but also the fastest solution since projects could be commissioned within three to four years from financial close. After whetting by all provinces the policy was approved by the Council of Common Interests and work on implementation began.

A month later, in September 2013, Nepra, the electric power regulatory authority, announced an upfront tariff on coal power projects. The aim was to help the project sponsors arrive at their investment decisions early and then achieve financial close on fast track. That not too many investment decisions were forthcoming, and the one that was, Engro Energy, was unable to achieve financial close, perhaps indicated that the tariff was too low. There was little wrong with Nepra's conservative approach. Often a 'reverse auction' of this sort is an effective method to arrive at fair pricing.

Of course there was the added complication of coal's deleterious climate effects. No worries, we justified to ourselves, because Pakistan's grid — thanks to the large share of natural gas and hydro power — is one of the cleanest in the world. Surely we could get away with a bit of coal in the mix. Western financial institutions had a different view. Coal was an absolute no-no. Their stakeholders would have none of it. At any rate, given the chronic circular debt malaise, global financial institutions had little appetite to invest in our power sector.

In the face of these roadblocks the government reached out to the Chinese leadership. A number of projects have been identified that can be jointly developed. These include, among others, two power plants each at Gadani, Sahiwal, Thar and one at Bin Qasim. A coal handling and logistics infrastructure is also part of the parcel as is a transmission infrastructure for evacuation of electricity from the site to the grid.

Amidst a global economic slowdown and the slack demand for coal power plants, Chinese power plant manufacturers didn't have too many orders either. A meeting point was possible if the Pakistan government enhanced the tariff somewhat and improved the rates of return; the projects would become viable to receive Chinese funding. In June this year, Nepra revised the tariff. To minimise the cost of capital, power projects need to be structured at around 80:20 debt-equity ratio. Chinese government financing could now be provided to cover the debt component.

One reservation that has been aired about the deal is of bypassing of the public procurement rules. These reservations are not valid for private-sector projects in IPP mode. Even for Gencos that may opt for retrofitting for coal conversion and for Greenfield projects involving federal/provincial government equity there is no harm if the government puts such projects under independent boards and empowers these boards to procure through direct negotiations while keeping the global industry benchmarks on cost per megawatt, efficiency and other key parameters in view.

This information is widely and freely available. To further address transparency concerns, negotiated proposals can be made the subject of public hearings before they are signed. The larger consideration is whether the policy objective of bringing down the weighted average cost of electricity production is being met. Another consideration should be that the equipment is of high quality and must perform up to the standard, unlike the earlier experience with Chinese locomotives.

But perhaps even more than capital cost, the mechanism to procure fuel supply contracts needs to be fully transparent because fuel is a recurring and 'pass through' cost — passed on to the government — and prices are harder to ascertain for coal than for furnace oil and natural gas.

Pakistan needs affordable energy. A course has been charted, and while differences in viewpoints can exist, issues must not be obfuscated for political gain.

LNG IMPORTS

September 2014

THE petroleum minister has described as a game changer an initiative to import Liquefied Natural Gas to fuel cars with CNG. Under the proposal the CNG pump operators can set up one or more special purpose vehicles (SPV) to import LNG, which would be re-gasified on arrival at the Port Qasim terminal facility presently under construction. It will then be piped to CNG stations countrywide through the leaky pipelines' infrastructure of the two gas utility companies.

The minister has claimed this would shave $2.5 billion off the oil import bill, make available a 35pc cheaper fuel for consumers and also save the sagging CNG industry.

That the initiative also proposes to exempt LNG imports from GST and the gas infrastructure development cess (GIDC) suggests that the rate differential between the landed costs of crude oil and LNG may not be very much. That in fact if these are applied, it may squeeze the profit margins of the CNG pump operators down to the bone. This also potentially belies the $2.5bn saving claim.

This is akin to providing a subsidy to a scheme that may not otherwise be viable. The petroleum ministry's argument that the imported LNG would free up gas that the CNG sector presently receives and this would then be diverted to the textile sector and independent power producers (IPP) where it would continue to yield taxes and the cess is fallacious and a distortion of competition.

While the measure may simultaneously placate PML-N's traditional constituencies — the textile lobby, IPP owners, CNG station owners and millions of vehicle owners — it violates the principle of neutrality of broad-based taxation. The principle states that GST is a tax on consumption, irrespective of the product being consumed, and is to be paid by the final consumer.

Similarly the cess is meant to be used on developing future gas infrastructure and it makes little sense to exempt LNG because at some stage, if demand picks up, more pipeline capacity would need to be built.

At least transparency and national accounting practices would be better served if the government were to levy the tax and cess with one hand and with the other give a direct cash subsidy to vehicle drivers buying CNG at the stations.

So why have the CNG pump operators, with their SPV and the best of intentions, been unable to make this scheme commercially viable? To comprehend this we need to understand that the international LNG trade is carried on between a closed club, where the buyers and sellers are blue chip entities with A or AA credit ratings. As such, entities with lower ratings should expect to receive less favourable terms.

There are 19 exporting countries, Qatar accounting for a third of global production; and 25 importing countries led by Japan, South Korea and Europe. A limited 400 special LNG tankers ply cargo, spanning the globe from Alaska to Australia, the typical cargo value being $200 million. Among these, smaller size vessels of cargo worth $30m to $80m are also available but buying in smaller lots pushes up the landed cost per unit.

Vessel charter rates are also highly volatile. A good part of the cost in this business is in the supply chain and the handling. Importantly, Qatar with its predisposition for larger cargoes, would mean the SPV will have to pick up cargo from more distant destinations which would further drive up its per unit landed cost.

Even once it arrives, a further 10pc of the gas will be lost (and become part of the unaccounted for gas losses) during distribution. The final price at the CNG pumps, including profit, may well be only a fraction lower than petrol — hence the proposal to exempt it from GST and cess.

A better option may be to capacitate PSO, the country's largest fuel importer, to handle LNG imports. PSO has a more robust financial position than any SPV the CNG pump operators will be able to come up with. It also has better experience of negotiating contracts, procurement procedures and can source much better deals. PSO will be able to achieve an economies effect and land the product at lower per unit prices.

It makes more sense for PSO to spin off a division to handle LNG requirements of all industrial sectors than for individual sectors to go it alone. The petroleum ministry must ask PSO to conduct a feasibility study on the opportunity.

Utmost, of course, systemic gas losses need to be plugged before piping expensive gas into it. This issue should be addressed head on rather than glossing over it by extending tax subsidies and distorting markets.

THE FUEL STORY

January 2015

ONE can tell a story from different starting points. And the story can be told from the perspective of different protagonists; in which each one will embellish their narrative to make them feel they are better people than they really are. And that is the sense one gets from watching the protagonists of the oil shortage saga on prime time television.

One thing is for sure. The crisis did not begin with petrol pumps in Punjab drying up.

And it will not end with the arrival of vessels bringing fresh supplies. In fact we may not see the back of this crisis for a long time. But a story has been spun to prevent us from getting to the bottom of this malaise.

For now, PSO (and the petroleum ministry) has been made the fall guy. This story begins on Jan 1 when after the price reduction the demand spiked; it was not foreseen and neither had sufficient supplies been arranged for. The tipping point had arrived at which a couple of million motorists would switch fuel from CNG to petrol.

The story went on that the oil marketing companies (OMCs) were required to carry statutory reserves. They did not. And Ogra, the oil and gas authority, failed to regulate or enforce. Ogra should have realised that OMCs and dealers will skimp on buying and holding stocks in a falling market. To make matters worse, a refinery went out of action for four days. Consumers went into panic, the media fuelled the frenzy. And the shortage arrived.

For the sake of argument, let's suppose PSO had been carrying three weeks of reserve. That the tipping point to switch from CNG had not arrived. The refinery hadn't tripped. Was all else well? Would the crisis not have happened, even if a few weeks later? Would PSO's cash flow position, its credit with banks and suppliers, its ability to sustain imports, have been in any better shape?

The story also does not explain why the furnace oil stocks depleted. Was there a spike in demand here too?

And this is where it starts running into problems of credibility. Surely there is more than is being told us.

Now with PSO as protagonist what is the story? Was PSO not crying out all of last year for its receivables due from the power sector to be paid because they were hampering its ability to import fresh stocks? How many times, in how many meetings and through how many letters was the issue raised?

Did the finance ministry and the cabinet's Economic Coordination Committee not foresee an impending supply chain disruption? The finance minister has stated it's not a "financial issue". Right.

The country cannot import fuel because LC limits have been maxed out and it's not a financial issue? What is a financial issue then?

So when they sat around the table, something had to give. A story had to be spun. One would be let off the hook. Another would apologise. A committee would be made as would a promise of fresh supplies in the days to come. End of story.

The character deleted from this story was the power sector. Furnace oil is what straddles the power and petroleum sectors. And this is really a furnace oil payment cycle crisis.

Furnace oil accounts for almost half of our fuel import bill. A third of all our electricity is generated by burning furnace oil. And while there is no crisis in other products which are sold on cash and on which PSO and other oil marketing companies make a neat profit margin, furnace oil is what causes them cash flow difficulties.

The previous PPP-led ruling coalition had pumped Rs1.5 trillion into the power sector to cover for losses caused by inefficiencies and theft.

But it could not muster the political capital necessary to undertake the painful power sector reform during its tenure, especially as oil prices were going through the roof. The present government injected another Rs500 billion at the start of its term into a sector that was hemorrhaging nearly Rs1bn a day. But because the root causes were not addressed, the hemorrhaging continued and it's piled up again.

Apart from the inability to pursue reform there is another story about institutional breakdown. And yet another about the management style of this government. But I will leave these for later.

What will happen now? A tranche will be released. Some or all of the circular debt of Rs600bn will be settled. Petrol supplies will resume.

Furnace oil will also be procured on emergency basis. We will tide over the immediate difficulty without addressing the underlying malaise. Until another story develops. More on that later.

LNG MUDDLE

May 2015

THE muddle that has been created with the Liquefied Natural Gas (LNG) project reflects both a lack of clear thinking as also clumsy planning and implementation. While much fuss has been made in the media about logistical difficulties, most of these could be put down to 'teething problems' allowing for a very generous definition of the term.

Essentially, the muddle is the cause of bad economics, not logistical difficulties.

The economics was very simple to work out, perhaps easier even than the logistics. Before the government embarked on the project it ought to have worked out who the LNG was for and at what price was it going to be offered. It should have looked at the cost of the present fuel to the user and how much saving LNG would bring.

Fuel-switching decisions are economic decisions. The question really was who would be willing to pay $14 per MMBTU for re-gasified LNG? Once we had identified potential takers the question of putting in a supply chain to meet demand was merely a technical one. Let's look at the major users of gas one by one.

The fertiliser sector uses it as feedstock and is presently being sold gas at the rate of $1-2 per MMBTU (Engro for even less). The domestic consumers receive it for between $1-3 depending on the slab the user falls into.

For decades, gas has been hugely underpriced in Pakistan and that has led to excessive and wasteful demand and it has served as a disincentive to new discovery because the financial reward does not justify the cost of prospecting.

The question of LNG apart, these prices need to be urgently reviewed as they are creating market distortions and leading to poor allocation of resources.

Then there is the CNG sector that gets gas at $6.5 per MMBTU. When oil prices were hovering above $100 per barrel (and on top of that petrol is heavily taxed) CNG pump operators could sell it at 60 or 70pc parity to petrol and still make a hefty profit.

The sharp decline in oil prices has changed that and now only a small rate differential remains between petrol and CNG price. This is despite much heavier taxes on petrol.

If the tax effects were to be levelled there is no question of the CNG sector being able to take up at the present $6.5 per MMBTU leave alone taking up LNG. The principle of neutrality in taxation states that the tax system should be neutral so choice-of-fuel decisions are made on economic merit and not for tax reasons. The Federal Board of Revenue should begin citing this principle when it attends inter-ministerial meetings on LNG pricing.

That only leaves the power sector as a potential taker of Liquefied Natural Gas. But before I go into that, there is another small muddle that needs to be cleared. There is talk of a 'basket price' for gas in some quarters — which would be the weighted average cost from all sources, imported and foreign.

Generally, under good accounting practices the fair value of a commodity is the cost of replacing every sold unit with a new unit. In our context, that replacement is done in two ways; either import or make new indigenous discoveries.

The import price is $14 per MMBTU landed at the customer's doorstep. Meanwhile, the government has offered a price of $6 for new gas discovery. When was the last time that negotiations were held with foreign companies to ask them to look for more gas? The two local companies OGDC and PPL are already owed billions of rupees from circular debt that originates in the power sector. With the local companies in that situation, how can foreign companies be motivated to undertake new discovery?

Other than new discovery there is another faster and shorter term solution. When a gas field begins to deplete, enhanced recovery processes — such as compressors — are used to pull out residual and tight gas. This involves capital investment and to offset that governments typically adjust wellhead prices upwards. There are a few gas fields where this can be done. But that would need some serious work in the petroleum ministry.

So coming back to the last category — the power sector — all the dozen or so Gencos's (which date back to before the 1994 IPP policy) are capable of being fired on natural gas. So are half a dozen of the more recent IPP's.

Pakistan should be able realise marginal savings on fuelling power generation if it can bring costs in the LNG supply chain down and neutrality in taxation should be applied by exempting GST on LNG for the power sector since furnace oil is already exempt.

THE GAS CHALLENGE

July 2015

NEWS of Iran reaching a landmark agreement with the big powers has once again invigorated talk of the Iran-Pakistan gas pipeline. The adviser to the prime minister on foreign affairs, Sartaj Aziz, has been reported as saying that once sanctions are lifted, Pakistan would move quickly to implement the agreement. On his part, the petroleum minister says that as soon as the sanctions are lifted, the pipeline would be built and Pakistan would receive gas from Iran. Now, if only the real world was that simple.

As I have mentioned in these columns before, the gas shortage and crisis in Pakistan is the cause of bad economics and not logistical difficulties or sanctions. And no matter how much gas is available at our doorstep, our domestic market will not be able to absorb it at international prices. We already have an LNG terminal which was intended to be importing gas at full capacity but is instead languishing.

All our gas-consuming sectors are addicted to low prices. These prices are centrally administered and do not reflect the true economic value of this scarce resource. Natural gas is used for both consumptive and productive purposes. Decades of economic decisions made on the basis of these centrally administered prices have resulted in a wasteful, inefficient and poor allocation of a valuable resource and discouraged fresh exploration activity. To redress this situation requires a radical shift away from administered prices to those based on fair economic value.

In that sense the impending inflow of gas at global prices represents an opportunity to rationalise gas prices. The recent sharp fall in world petroleum prices means this can be done less painfully. Still, domestic gas prices are a fraction of international prices. And incremental increases like the government seems to be doing will not do the trick.

A quick and dirty solution would be to simply mix the imported gas with the local and then calculate a weighted average basket price. That would exacerbate, not address the existing economic distortions. Hopefully, the government does not want to go down that road and this was made apparent last year when in a highly publicised press conference, the petroleum minister had announced that the CNG sector would take up some of the imported LNG. The CNG sector has not had much success with this. The overarching reason may be because the price of imported gas is roughly twice the administered price of $6.5 per mmbtu at which this sector has been receiving domestic gas. This was not something that was too difficult to foresee. In the absence of fair value pricing, the government is unable to arrive at the conclusion that CNG may not after all, be a viable fuel to substitute motor petrol.

The domestic sector gets its gas at even less, a tiny fraction of the international price. And each time gas prices have been raised, so the rate of theft has also gone up. In some distribution regions half the gas is stolen as consumers chisel clumsy holes in the pipeline and use rubber pipes to run stoves and heaters. And even as they siphon off the required three or four units per day, the larger rupture often leads to perhaps another 97 units leaking into the atmosphere. Both the gas utility companies are unable and unwilling to plug the losses.

The remedial measure in this situation would be to turn off natural gas supply in high-theft areas and instead shift to providing LPG cylinders which is a main cooking and heating fuel in many developing countries. Cheap gas is also serving as a deterrent to the uptake of solar water heating and one wonders if subsidy can be given on gas then why it cannot be given for the one-time installation of solar water heating apparatus to low-income households.

Fertiliser production is another problematic area where according to some estimates the government is giving away more in gas subsidy to fertiliser manufacturers than if it were to simply subsidise imported fertiliser. An added irony is that Pakistani farmers pay more for urea fertiliser than farmers in neighbouring countries.

In the final analysis, power generation may be the only sector that uses gas productively. (Though even here there have been reports of K-Electric, under its present management, pilfering gas in running its Bin Qasim plant.) At any rate, the government must immediately develop and present its future gas road map which then it must implement in the two-year lead time it takes to construct the IP pipeline. That is if another LNG terminal story is to be avoided. Indeed, without that road map the government may have trouble raising finance for the pipeline.

WIND POWER

August 2015

IN many countries, wind energy now forms a substantial portion of energy production. In Pakistan, excepting three projects of total 150MW, we have not been able to make a go of it. A few years ago the Alternate Energy Development Board (AEDB) prepared a wind energy development plan. This targeted 3,000MW by 2016 and 5,000MW by 2020.

Now, there are three reasons why this is not happening: 1) Even if wind power plants are planned, we have the rather anomalous situation where the grid in the Jhimpir wind corridor does not have sufficient capacity to take in more power; 2) the constant tinkering with tariffs offered has put off many investors; and 3) the unnecessary and complicated red tape around the process for obtaining wind power generation licenses from Nepra, the national power regulator, deters many applicants who have reasons to believe that licenses are only granted to political favourites. These bottlenecks are above and beyond the largest commercial impediment to investment in any power generation business in Pakistan: circular debt.

Meanwhile in southern Sindh, tens of thousands of acres of rich wind potential are lying desolate in what should have been operational wind farms of all types and sizes. Adjacent to one of the world's largest mega cities, this is not some remote unreachable area. In addition there is thousands of megawatts of additional potential offshore. In contrast, India has installed 24,000MW of wind power across Tamil Nadu, Maharashtra, Gujarat and Rajasthan. This is more than Pakistan's total installed capacity from all sources and represents 10pc of India's total power generation capacity.

So assuming there is political will, can there be a fast track plan to harness 3,000MW in, say, the next three years? The answer is a resounding yes. But for that, the multitude of power-sector organisations would have to align their objectives. They currently seem to be working at cross-purposes. The ministry of water and power needs to put the sequence straight. Briefly, that would require 1) the national transmission and dispatch company (NTDC) to urgently undertake a massive upgrade of grid infrastructure (its current plan of 500MW upgrade is grossly insufficient). Power evacuation is guaranteed under the power policy, there is no excuse for government failure on this count. 2) Nepra should fix a realistic and reasonable upfront tariff; and following this, it can 3) adopt a liberal licensing policy and let project sponsors find ways to develop viable projects while working within this tariff figure.

To save time, Nepra ought to grant a license (if a licensee fulfills all other conditions) even if the grid capacity currently does not exist. On granting the license it should advise NTDC to ensure the necessary grid capacity in the two years it takes for project financial close and construction. For this the NTDC should be provided funds and if it is still unable to complete the job then it can be made liable for penalty payments till the date power evacuation begins. This would remove the uncertainty and clear the way for projects to proceed.

Another opportunity is the arrangement known as wheeling, where a power producer in one location could sell electricity to a bulk consumer in another, while paying a tolling fee to the NTDC. Again the provision for this exists in the power policy but the ministry of water and power has been unable to make this work in the last two years. This policy should be made operational immediately and Nepra should penalise any distribution company (DISCO) found falling short.

This series of steps would remove the major impediments after which AEDB can be given the target to achieve 3,000MW in new projects in the next three years — that is, if the PML-N government is serious about its pledge of ending power outages, or load-shedding, as we like to call it. I raise the question because I have on more than one occasion heard talk among the wind power investment community of the current political government's lack of enthusiasm for Sindh's wind potential, preferring instead to prioritise the solar initiative in Cholistan and LNG-fuelled power projects in Punjab. I hope this talk is merely banter.

The latest State Bank of Pakistan report indicates that foreign direct investment (FDI) has all but dried up and is down to $700 million in the last fiscal. This reflects more a lack of imagination and capacity than any external challenge. As shown, once the objectives are aligned and things are put in the correct order, $5 billion in FDI can be attracted in the wind power sector alone. I will ask the question one more time: does the PML-N government have the will?

SOLAR POWER DEBATE

September 2015

THE PML-N government once again finds itself amidst a needless controversy; this time over the 100MW project at the Quaid-i-Azam solar park in Bahawalpur. And while this may partly be the consequence of loud and boisterous claims of ending the power crisis, and for which there has been little action, it largely reflects the PML-N government's failure to manage public expectations.

The story that should have been told at the very outset was simple: the world over, solar power is the fastest-growing resource for renewable energy. This trend is being driven by a steep decline in the cost of solar panels — whose cost has dropped to one-third in the last five years.

Compared to this — according to the US Energy Information Administration — equipment cost of wind power has come down by half, while the cost of nuclear capacity has declined by 20pc and thermal by 10pc in the last five years. Going forward, costs of solar are expected to decline still further, and at a faster rate than other technologies.

The time had come for Pakistan to enter the game. It needed to acquire the technology and build the technological ecosystem for its widespread adoption. The first project would be a demonstration project that the Punjab government would itself undertake. This would remove the risk for subsequent projects. Even though the cost of electricity would be high at this stage, subsequent projects will ride the declining cost curve and deliver cheaper power.

In 2012, Pakistan had similarly entered the game of wind power and experienced a similar effect. End of story. This could have been published as a policy document and given widespread circulation to pre-empt any controversy.

The PML-N lost another opportunity when last week, to rebut the criticisms in the media, the chief minister of Punjab addressed a news conference. In this he termed it the 'most viable venture in the country' and claimed it to be more cost effective than wind energy. (In fact the reverse is true. This is the most expensive electric power in the country.)

In support of his claim he quoted the capital cost of $1.33 million per megawatt for solar and compared it to $2.1m for wind power. This is obfuscation at its best. What was not mentioned was that you get only half the output from each installed megawatt of solar (plant factor 17.5 pc) as compared to wind (plant factor 35 pc).

Effectively then, it takes 2MW of solar capacity — and a cost of $2.66m — to get the same energy you would from 1MW of installed capacity of wind power — which would cost $2.1m. This makes solar photovoltaic technology 27pc more expensive than wind on 'output from installed capacity' basis.

A more straightforward comparison would have been between the levellised upfront tariff being offered by the electric power regulator Nepra — 14 cents per unit for solar projects and 10.6 cents for wind. If, as the Punjab chief minister claims, the cost of solar is cheaper than wind, then why should solar power be 32pc more expensive?

Two days after Shahbaz Sharif's news conference in Lahore, Sindh's provincial ministers Murad Ali Shah and Nisar Khuhro in Karachi accused the federal government of obstructing the development of wind power projects in Sindh. They also questioned the ban imposed by the federal government on wind power projects and why it was reluctant to build grid capacity to evacuate power from these projects.

These are valid concerns which the federal government should note. A potential 3,000MW of power projects (and arguably over $5 billion in FDI) is currently choked because of this one single bottleneck. The PML-N federal government ought to embrace these national projects instead of being seen to be obstructing them.

In his news conference, the Punjab chief minister went on to suggest that over the years, solar power production would rival that from hydro. This was a ludicrous claim to make. Hydroelectricity contributes 30pc (or nearly 7,000 MW) of Pakistan's total electricity demand; and that percentage is likely to increase as new dams are built at Diamer-Bhasha, Bunji and Dasu.

Under Pakistan's energy vision, solar (and wind) will always remain marginal while the base load will be carried by thermal and nuclear plants. Hydropower will remain a major contributor. Even then, it will be years before the solar cost curve can drop tariffs to the level of say the 8.5 cents per unit that was offered to the recently completed hydro-power IPP, Laraib Energy.

That said, solar is a long-term strategic play and I have previously supported its development in these columns. Instead of tit-for-tat rebuttals, Shahbaz Sharif should explain his case more from the strategic vantage point suggested above.

A SMART CHOICE?

October 2015

IF you air-condition your house in the hot months, you would probably fall in the billing slab where you pay above Rs19 for each unit. Offices and commercial premises would pay more. These are high rates, even compared to what your peer consumers in countries far richer than Pakistan would be paying.

The trouble with domestic production of solar electricity used to be its high cost. Most electricity consumers were also deterred by the perceived difficulties of installing and maintaining a rooftop solar system. An additional question was that while you could produce electricity in the daytime on your rooftop, what would happen at night? Setting up a battery system would cost more than the solar system itself. The result: we have seen almost nonexistent uptake of solar energy in Pakistan. That may now be about to change. The buck is with the utilities — the 10 or so distribution companies (DISCOS) across Pakistan.

My last article had observed that we have recently seen a steep decline in the cost of solar panels which have come down to a third of what they were five years ago. Solar power experts put today's estimated figure at Rs15 per unit (levelised cost over the life of the rooftop system). This falls below the grid parity price of Rs19. It also hedges you against future increases in the price of electricity.

The other significant development has been the recent notification by the electric power regulator Nepra, of the 'Alternative & Renewable Energy, Distributed Generation and Net Metering Regulations'. This means a framework now exists whereby consumers can generate solar power on their rooftops and after their use, feed any surplus electricity to the grid. A 'Smart', reversible meter would be installed at the customer premises which during feed in would run in reverse mode. At other times you may be drawing electricity, such as at night time.

At the end of the month the meter will give a 'net' reading. This scheme simultaneously dispenses with the need for storage batteries while substantially reducing the number of electricity units households draw from the grid. Conceivably this could also result in the consumer falling in a lower billing slab where they may be charged say Rs15 for each unit drawn instead of Rs19.

On paper, all this augurs very well for the take-off finally, of the solar power generation opportunity to which Pakistan can finally turn to in a substantial way. It would bring down electricity demand from the grid particularly air conditioning during daytime and office hours while contributing some additional electricity to the grid which would reduce the requirement to build imported fuel-based power plants. The Alternate Energy Development Board estimates that 2000-3000 MW can be brought into the system this way. And while Pakistan's is a relatively low emissions grid, this would make it greener still. The resulting reduction in emissions can be converted to carbon credits that the utilities can monetise.

However, as it trends towards a happy ending, there is a twist in the story. None of the DISCOS, the utility companies, are ready. If tomorrow, hundreds of net metering applications were to be received, they have no way of processing them. No procedures, no systems and no technical and personnel capacity. That is the sad truth and Nepra's recently released annual report 2014-15 confirms the sorry state of affairs at all the utility companies.

Second there is the issue of grid instability, mainly the problem of the hours of power outages during which time the grid would not be available to take in any excess capacity from the rooftop system. This would adversely affect the returns and payback calculations, reducing incentive.

Third is the utilities' fear that their best paying and most lucrative segments of customers would attrite. There would be natural resistance and that is a paradox for the bureaucrats of the Ministry of Water and Power to resolve.

Perhaps a good template to pick up would be the Dubai Electricity and Water Authority's recently launched Shams initiative. It provides detailed guidelines and processes on implementing such a scheme and considerable thought appears to have gone into devising it. Customers would only need to turn to a panel of consultants, contractors and equipment manufacturers whom the utility would have pre-qualified to interface with customers and also undertake most of the work on the utilities' behalf. To keep transaction costs to a minimum, most of the application process is online.

The Alternate Energy Distributed Generation and Net Metering Regulations were first proposed by AEDB in 2012. It has taken Nepra's bureaucracy another three years to notify. It should now not take the utilities more years before these are implemented.

ENERGY CORRIDOR

November 2015

CLIMATE and topography bequeath Central Asia with rich hydropower potential. After heavy winter snowfall come the strong sun and warm summers. This brings melting water, 40 cubic kilometres each year, down from glaciers in the Tian Shan Mountains and snowfields in the highlands and steppe land.

As it comes down Kyrgyzstan's 40,000 rivers and streams, the water drops thousands of metres in altitude. Further south, Tajikistan's mountains and rivers provide it an estimated 4pc of the world's hydropower resources. There is surplus electricity in the summer months and now a plan — known as CASA 1000 — is to export 1300MW to Pakistan and Afghanistan

Both countries have reached an agreement under which Afghanistan will receive a fee of 1.25 cents per kWh from Pakistan in exchange for letting 1000MW transit through its territory. The power purchase price is reported to be five cents. This does not appear to be a bad deal for Pakistan.

The shortage of electricity in this country is an impediment to greater industrialisation. A plan to establish a series of industrial estates along the path of the China-Pakistan Economic Corridor had to be shelved this year for want of electricity. Power generation is not the only constraint. A ramshackle transmission and distribution system is equally to blame. Consider for example Sindh's wind corridor where against 4000MW of immediate wind power potential the grid is unable to evacuate anything close to that from Jhimpir where the wind estates are located. Most of the potential is being squandered.

After reaching Kabul from Tajikistan, the planned CASA 1000 transmission line will enter Pakistan at Torkham before reaching Peshawar. What arrangements are being planned to then transmit this 1000MW to other parts of the country? How can we be sure that we will then not encounter another Sindh wind corridor type situation?

At the same time, I ought to point out a couple of potential risks. Kyrgyzstan and Tajikistan also have decrepit, Soviet-era grids that struggle to keep the lights on. If, like us they also plan to upgrade their grid in the coming years and there is a surge in domestic demand, could we expect a curtailment in electricity available for export? Second, many of the Soviet-era dams are in need of rehabilitation, while new ones are also planned. To what extent is the project predicated on the investments that are going to be made here and what are the risks if these do not materialise? Lastly, there is the risk is of escalating insurgency in Afghanistan.

Nonetheless, energy arbitrage is only one aspect of this project. Its bigger component is improving regional connectivity and economic integration between Kyrgyzstan, Tajikistan, Afghanistan and Pakistan. Such projects create interdependencies and give the countries a stake in each other's stability and security.

The planned Tapi gas pipeline is another such project. That takes a different route as it enters Afghanistan from Turkmenistan, north of Herat and then takes a circuitous course along the Afghanistan ring road to arrive at Kandahar before crossing over to Quetta.

The Iran Pakistan gas pipeline is yet another. The same region is traversed by a North-South highway that links the Iranian port of Chabahar with the Afghanistan ring road. This too is an access to Central Asia. The Afghanistan segment of this road is Indian-built and a cause of much (and needless) chagrin in Pakistani defence quarters.

To be clear, it was Pakistan's intransigence — and not too bright a move on the chessboard — of not allowing India overland transit to Iran and Afghanistan, which led to Chabahar's development. Were it not for that there would today be a strong commercial lobby in India pressing for harmonious relations with Pakistan.

Beyond energy resources Afghanistan holds substantial deposits of high quality iron ore and coking coal in its Bamiyan province and in which, a few years ago, a consortium of Indian companies had obtained over $10 billion in mining concessions.

Through these columns, let me float the idea for this ore and coal to be brought by means of a straight 600km rail line that can be laid from Bamiyan running through Miramshah in North Waziristan and down to Kalabagh. A giant steel mill could be established here, possibly with Russian assistance that would supply steel products to industries in northern Pakistan and the states of western India.

Crowning all these initiatives, of what could become a mesh of electricity transmission lines, gas pipelines, mines, roads, railways and ports, is the China Pakistan Economic Corridor.

Energy, steel, ports, transit corridors and human capital are the primary resources on which nations are built. We have all the building blocks in sight. The only thing needed is a vision that transcends zero-sum thinking.

ECONOMIC DEVELOPMENT

Besides the effects of the war on terror, energy shortages and regional isolation what else plagues Pakistan's underdevelopment? This section explores a few more themes.

FOUR STRENGTHS TO BUILD ON

May 2009

ON the eve of September 11, 2001, the country was a pariah state under a military ruler — impoverished, bankrupt, a source of proliferating nuclear technology and a state using jihadis to further its regional territorial interests.

The 1990s had ended as what many termed a "lost decade" in which a population bomb had exploded. Seven years and $10bn after 9/11, there is enormous international goodwill. There is noise and chaos of a democracy.

Following the inflating and bursting of a real estate and stock market asset bubble, the economy is again in despair. A double game has ended as a political consensus appears to be developing against Islamic militancy. Large parts of the NWFP are still outside government control.

Since 9/11, 30 million people have been born — a generation that risks a strong probability of witnessing in their lifetimes, cataclysmic events of a type only their ancestors would have seen a century earlier, that fateful summer of 1947 when "...violence spread from one part of Lahore to another like a plague. There must have been trained gangs of thugs moving from one place to another. It was hard to reconcile these bloody events with the nature of our life in pre-partition Lahore," writes celebrated Indian painter Krishen Khanna in a piece for the book Beloved City: Writings on Lahore edited by Bapsi Sidhwa.

"No one could have imagined that entire populations would be bludgeoned out and rendered homeless and such cruelty and barbarity would prevail amongst Punjabis," Khanna, a blue-blooded Lahori who studied at Government College and spent many childhood days in the shadow of Kim's Gun in front of the Lahore Museum, tells us. No one probably imagined it on the eve of partition in 1947, and no one can today imagine the possibility of such a scenario erupting again in, say, 2047. Luckily for Khanna, the process of partition ended. He was able to revisit Lahore in 1988 during the First International Biennale of Arts and sketch the cannon in drawings and abstract paintings. On the other hand, the crisis towards which we are now headed does not have a happy ending.

A regional scramble for water is set to begin — with the Himalayan glacial melt — that begins in as little as 10 years from now. The country will have yet another 30 million people by that time. A predicted deluge, followed by water shortages, desertification, and climate refugees are only some of the expected outcomes. Pakistan is going to be hit hard. By some accounts the Cholistan desert is expected to expand — reaching to the outskirts of Sahiwal.

In the interest of its people, Pakistan will need to enter this very challenging era as a significant economic and military power. After losing the last two decades, the next 10 years probably represent the last window of opportunity. Pakistan will need to urgently build on four of its existing strengths if it is to stand a fighting chance of survival in the several difficult decades beginning as early as 2020.

The first of these strengths is the mountain of international goodwill that presently exists for Pakistan. This will not last forever. This is an opportunity for Pakistan to harness this tide in its own favour to position itself as a significant player for the power politics of the water scramble that lies ahead. Put bluntly, Pakistan needs to look beyond seeking handouts that barely keep its head above the water. Regardless of assurances that "we wronged you and we will not walk away" this window is open only for a while. In a fast-changing world, no US administration can guarantee what future US interests and priorities will be.

In the larger scheme of things, a Pakistan that is unable to take back control of its territory from non-state actors and deny its soil for their activities will find this goodwill beginning to evaporate. It will find it hard to justify possessing and holding on to its nuclear weapons. In time the world may well find a solution to resolve this dilemma. A Pakistan without nuclear weapons in which Islamic militant and other vigilante groups and warlords control dwindling water resources will not be a worry for the United States. It will not be a worry for a powerful next-door India that will be able to trample on the Indus water treaty in the absence of a credible state.

The military is conscious of the fact that the activities of militant Islamists can degrade the capacity of the state to function; it can injure society and impose unacceptable costs on the economy. This ultimately depletes the nation's economic and war potential. It is also conscious that Pakistan's perception as a declining power would make it a less attractive partner for the US, France, Iran and even China.

A wise old man who lives on top of a mountain once said "Carry a big stick, but speak softly." In this sense, our nuclear arsenal (together with a powerful military) represents the second strength. In terms of a packing list for the future, we will need this big stick when the water scramble begins. We will not need the Taliban. Clearly, therefore, Pakistan had to make a choice between its Islamists and its nuclear arsenal. At last week's APC, it chose correctly.

The third strength is this country's energy, agriculture and trade corridor potential — representing an opportunity to develop the economic elements of national power. Pakistan has to get to work on developing its Thar coal assets — using clean coal technologies. Seawater agriculture is an emerging technology that needs to be explored. In agriculture, high-value crops, improvement of soil carbon content, efficient irrigation technologies and forestation along canals should be priority areas when asking our friends to help.

Our fourth strength is a nascent, imperfect and chaotic democracy, one that is dominated by flawed but still, relatively secular parties. Pakistan must consolidate its present gains and evolve its imperfect political system and culture into democratic institutions that are able to deliver what Political Science 101 says a political system should determine who gets what, when, where, how and why. Impressively Pakistan's "fragile" democracy has addressed at least one question correctly, when it built a consensus for Pakistan to fight back.

For the two riparian neighbours — both military and economic powers — water wars will be averted by domestic economic factors as much as the strength of their democracies. Domestic conflict will be averted by strengthening, particularly last-mile delivery, of governance and the distribution of public goods. This window is open for a while only. The post Taliban era must soon begin. There is a lot of work ahead.

A TALE OF TWO CITIES

June 2009

AS two lovely looking girls riding bicycles overtook us, I saw one of them turn to us, then say something to the other. They both giggled as they rode away. Having travelled more than my fair share, the novelty of visiting exciting places had diminished with each successive destination — until I arrived here.

I had never envisioned a place like this. Last week I visited Lahore. On the Mall road people courteously gave way to each other and smiled frequently. I saw nobody talk on a mobile phone nor heard any ring tones. There were bookshops and newspaper stalls but no hawkers nor any beggars. People waited patiently in lines at the theatres. There were far fewer people too and elegantly dressed, as if a dress code went into force in the evenings. There were many neatly managed wide open spaces with art deco. This was a fashionable and cosmopolitan city that had acquired the title of 'the Paris of India'. Last week I visited Lahore, as it was on the eve of the breakout of the Second World War.

In his book Lahore A Sentimental Journey, Pran Nevile takes the reader to the Lahore of his childhood and subsequently his days as a student at Government College. So with Nevile as my tourist guide I experienced craft shops and elegant cafes, met his friends, watched puppeteers perform on the street, strolled through a flower show at Lawrence Gardens and past the ballroom of the gymkhana where a waltz was in session.

The highlight was the ride in a tonga from Anarkali towards the Tollinton market, on which the greatest tourist attraction is Ahmad Shah Abdali's cannon, the Zamzama. Made of copper and brass I learnt how it sowed terror amongst the ranks of the Marhattas in the battle of Panipat in 1761. It was during one of Abdali's plundering expeditions to India that the gun was seized by Ranjit Singh and immortalised by Rudyard Kipling as Kim's Gun. It was said that whosoever owned this gun ruled Punjab.

We rode past K.L Mehra, tailors, the YMCA, Lloyds Bank and the telegraph office. Getting off the tonga, we walked past a theatre before coming on to Temple Road where children were playing with earthenware toys, a group of girls was playing hopscotch while some boys played gullie danda, a fascinating game requiring quick reflexes and exceptional hand-eye coordination. In the ante room of the newly opened Standard restaurant I picked up a copy of the Civil and Military Gazette and later, over dinner, joined a discussion with the intellectuals and glitterati of the day.

Amongst the people I met was Abdus Salam, a reserved, unremarkable youth whose father wanted him to take a job as a clerk in the government of the Raj "so the boy could make a life for himself". Not known to me and to the boy's father was that Salam had other dreams ... of becoming a physicist.

Lahore was pillaged by Mahmud of Ghazni, then plundered by the hordes of Genghis Khan, then razed by the Mongols. After this the reins of the city passed to the Mughal dynasty, heralding a dazzling age of splendour.

From here, Ranjit Singh lifted Lahore to the height of its celestial glory as the capital of the most powerful Punjabi kingdom there has ever been. Then during the British Raj the city witnessed an unprecedented era of peace and prosperity — as well as administration and laws — a welcome change after the Sikha shahi or arbitrary rule of the earlier dominions. I came to envy many aspects of Nevile's life and indeed his Lahore, built as it was on three layers that were still intact. Intact until the city was once again plundered by postcolonial failure, ravaged by the worst aspects of globalisation and razed by a population bomb.

So, by contrast, the Lahore I got in the flesh had obtrusive push-cart vendors, tasteless billboards, telecom towers atop unsightly buildings, and plastic bags and bottles littered everywhere. Sixty years of 'development' brought the noise of transport over the wall into our receding gardens as a permanent haze of smog blocked the sky. It introduced alien, inappropriate and heat-trapping architectural forms, designs and materials.

I have to admit that coming back from Pran's Lahore to mine was a bit of a culture shock. One day while negotiating a traffic snarl and visible road rage outside the Civil Secretariat, I recalled how in his day the Mall was sprayed with mist every evening to cool the temperature and settle the dust. In this moment I became aware not only of how quickly the cultural layers built by the Mughals, Ranjit Singh and the British were crumbling to ash but how even history had been rewritten in the name of a religious nationalism. My sentiment here is somewhat simplistic. By distorting history you are lying to children. You build a dishonest foundation.

Every day we hear the same cliché where are we headed? Let's also come to terms with where we are coming from. A sage once told me that you will find the answer — to where a nation is headed — in two places by listening carefully to what its old and wise are saying, and by looking at the present state of its youth. So I turned to Zia Mohyeddin and this is what I heard him say "... what I see around is deterioration of everything not just political life, which is obvious, but the deterioration of taste which I suppose is a natural corollary. I do not find encouraging signs ... and I don't mean in my own profession but about life. I find that people are less kind to each other than they used to be. I find, as I said, deterioration all around. I can't do anything about it. I can't make compromises now. So the best thing is ... well, to live in seclusion."

Out of Pran Nevile's Government College walked out Har Gobind Korana, Nobel laureate in molecular biology. He was followed by that dreamy youth I had figuratively met, Abdus Salam, Nobel laureate in physics. All eyes have been on its gates since then. Several dry decades have passed but none other has walked out.

It's been a week since I put the book down but one thought has not stopped nagging me. If the government of the Raj could teach its subjects to invent new knowledge, what insecurity drives an independent republic to imprison its children in an invented version of history?

TWO DIFFERENT PATHS

July 2009

IN the early 20th century the British-American Tobacco Company knew that a hookah-smoking Indian population would gradually switch to cigarettes. Towards the middle of the century Anglo-Dutch Unilever came to the same realisation that its banaspati could displace more traditional cooking mediums such as desi ghee and mustard oil.

Things moved slowly then. Clunky old lorries would bring the goods from the port or factory. Bullock carts would take them down shantytown lanes and dusty village tracks and finally skinny barebacked porters pulling wooden handcarts would deliver shop to shop. Today every major international retail brand and chain eyes the Indian market. Marks and Spencer has 12 stores in India and local chains such as Godrej Lifespace boasts 50 home and interiors stores offering furniture, appliances, health and massage products, digital cameras and other lifestyle products. Interestingly, their home range includes electronic security systems, vault equipment and burglary resistant safes.

Despite the retail temptation offered by the shopping malls, multiplexes, gyms, spas, restaurants and travel packages, Indian households still manage to save over a quarter of their disposable incomes, one of the highest rates in the region. By habit or custom, a large part of their accumulated savings is held in gold. In this way, Indian households accumulate 800 tons of gold each year — representing 20 per cent of the world's demand for gold — to store which Godrej has to sell a lot of vaults and safes!

The Indian household has also learnt that in bearish economic times, gold prices peak. Accordingly, in times of bust or drought, many opt to sell the gold and buy other low-priced assets. In the absence of an institutional mechanism, households turn to their nearest jeweller.

In a country with as many mobile phones as people and a 3 G licence auction months away, a sharp entrepreneur saw an opportunity. Jignesh Shah has created an Internet-based electronic spot market for gold. Now households can obtain prices and transact online. His company, the National Spot Exchange, had already done this for a number of other commodities including agricultural produce, eliminating the ageless institution of the middleman. With the resulting documentation, electronic commodity exchanges bring money from the informal economy into the banking system.

In turn, the Indian central bank has mandated the commercial banks to lend to the agriculture sector. This has created a strong demand from a flourishing rural sector creating a virtuous cycle that drives Indian industry and urban employment. Today India's forex reserves hover around $240bn and each year IT exports bring in $60bn into the economy. Meanwhile non-resident Indians or NRIs, by sending their savings, and often themselves, home — are the largest foreign investors in India. In the current fiscal year India will spend a luxurious $29bn on defence.

The day it placed an order for eight Boeing P-8I maritime reconnaissance planes, Boeing shares rose 27 cents. The P81 is the most advanced anti-submarine and anti-surface warfare aircraft in the world today. Its capability to watch India's coastline and maritime waters is undoubted. The defence budget includes $10bn for a next generation fighter jet, a mouth-watering contract for which both Boeing and Lockheed are competing.

The second item on the shopping list is the Aegis combat system. This is an integrated system that uses powerful computers and radars to track and destroy enemy targets and is only in use by the most advanced navies in the world. Just as Jagdish Shah's electronic commodity exchange is modernising an ancient system of trade, so will Aegis move the Indian navy into electronic warfare mode.

Today US defence equipment manufacturers represent a powerful lobby for India on Washington's Capitol Hill. They are interested in India's shopping list for the same reason British American tobacco was interested in the hookah-smoking village headman, commercial capitalism. Even the civilian nuclear deal extended by the US is primarily intended for American companies to win an estimated $100bn in consulting and contracting opportunities in India. All purchases are paid for in cold cash.

"History will be the ultimate judge of Pakistan," Jinnah had said at the time of partition. Whilst history may be some years away, it appears that the Indian defence establishment has begun preparations to firewall the country against a "rogue-state-failed-state next door" scenario. The measures include acquiring the capability, by 2015, to take down any incoming ballistic missiles. Accordingly the third item on the shopping list is a ballistic missile defence system, like the Patriot Advanced Capability-3.

Bollywood star Shilpa Shetty and business tycoon Mukesh Ambani both own cricket teams which the Indian Premier League brings, together with glamour and thrill under the media spotlight. And while Ratan Tata acquires British carmaker Land Rover and Jaguar he also gets ready to launch the world's smallest car, the Nano. The country has learnt to create wealth and now needs to give it time to work during which India is expected to invest $500bn in the next few years on upgrading its infrastructure.

Much as Godrej Lifespace sells electronic security systems and safes to increasingly affluent Indian households, the Indian security establishment appears to want to throw a security cordon around the country so that within it a secular and democratic Indian polity can get to work at addressing two internal challenges to better distribute the wealth that is being created and to improve social inclusiveness within Indian society.

How did the two countries end up on such different trajectories?

While there may be several answers to that, V.S. Naipaul, writing 10 years ago had spoken of a growing intellectual distance between the Hindus who embraced the New Learnings of Europe brought by the British Raj, and "the Muslims, who, wounded by their loss of power, and religious scruples, stood aside. This distance has grown with independence; and it is this — even more than religion now — that makes India and Pakistan quite distinct countries. India, with an intelligentsia that grows by leaps and bounds, expands in all directions. Pakistan, proclaiming only the faith and then proclaiming the faith again, ever shrinks".

FLOOD AFTERMATH

August 2010

ON the night of Nov 12, 1970, Cyclone Bhola — one of the worst natural disasters in recorded history — struck the shores of former East Pakistan. Around 350,000 lives were lost. With damage estimated at $86m (inflation adjusted to $1bn today) relief was slow to arrive.

The government of Yahya Khan came under severe criticism from Bengali leaders and from the local and international press. This Category 3 hurricane and its aftermath were to change the course of history.

This time the Indus River basin, a cradle of ancient civilisations and one of the world's largest natural resource has been the scene of a human catastrophe. Prime Minister Gilani has already termed the situation as being beyond the capacity of the government alone. This is indeed true. The damage to infrastructure alone has been staggering, with roads, bridges, power plants, refineries, dams, barrages and the irrigation system damaged across all four provinces, Azad Kashmir and Gilgit-Baltistan.

In a snap, 750,000 destroyed and damaged houses have been added to the national housing backlog of 7.5 million units. With some 1,600 dead and 14 million displaced, millions others are at risk of infections and waterborne diseases. Further beyond, tens of millions stand to lose their meagre capital and means of livelihood as crops and livestock are destroyed, markets do not operate, shops collapse and transport and communications come to a standstill.

In Khyber Pakhtunkhwa, Information Minister Mian Iftikhar Hussain estimates early losses at $2bn whilst Chief Minister Azam Khan Hoti terms this the worst natural disaster that has pushed back the province by 50 years. In Sindh and Punjab, the mainstay agricultural industry has been decimated. Crops and livestock spread over 1.6m acres in Punjab's agricultural heartland have been destroyed. While cotton and rice have already been affected, farmers may not be able to sow their next season crops as their cash cycle is interrupted. Meanwhile, according to the United Nations World Food programme, 80 per cent of the food reserves have been wiped out.

In recent years, Pakistan's agricultural growth has been stagnant. In renewed circumstances, and with the number of districts inundated, the sector could potentially contract by three to four per cent. With agriculture and livestock contributing 21 per cent to the national economy this could translate to 0.7 per cent being knocked off from the already low 4.5 per cent targeted GDP growth rate this year.

Losses, however, are not likely to remain confined to the crop and livestock sector but may extend to the value-added agro-processing sector like cotton ginning, rice milling and milk processing and also affect derived demand for seed, fertilisers and pesticide. This consequent ripple effect may chip off another half to three quarters of a percentage point from the GDP or approximately $1bn in absolute terms. The resulting supply side contraction has in fact already started to fuel inflation at a precarious time when Pakistan is struggling to stimulate economic growth.

Losses to infrastructure could translate to tens of billions of rupees in lost productivity and reconstruction costs. Finally the costs of relief operations and subsequent resettlement would also have to be borne by the exchequer. Together these costs will further balloon the fiscal deficit. With Islamabad already struggling, this consequence would make the chances of meeting the conditionalities appear even more remote as it meets the IMF's board in Washington to convince it to release the next two tranches of $1.3bn each.

All this while, the threat from faith-based terror and insurgent groups continues to loom as they evolve tactics and open new fronts in a war being fought for control of the state. The newest of these would be on the charity front, where in pursuit of a hidden agenda, a stray ideology will seek to undertake fundraising and relief operations and exploit the state's failing.

There may be temptations to channel the assistance already in the pipeline towards the flood emergency. While expedient, this course would detract from this aid's original objectives, which have been well thought out. De-prioritising these earlier objectives would therefore be unwise. Instead, this is the time for our friends to step forward to help a country — a member of the international community — that has been the largest contributor of troops to UN peacekeeping missions around the world. A new multibillion dollar assistance package would need to target three urgent needs one, relief operations through genuine charities and state organs; two, aid to farmers through innovative microfinance to restore their economic bases; and three, support for the Public Sector Development Programme and other programmes for the reconstruction of damaged infrastructure.

Of course there are three major challenges with mobilising such large-scale assistance. First, where will the money come from amidst a tight global financial environment? Second, how long will the process of allocation and subsequent disbursement take? Third, is there demonstrable and credible capacity available with the federal and provincial governments to effectively utilise these funds for the purposes and within the time frame intended? Each challenge can take months to address.

On the other hand, if the assistance does not materialise soon, then nearly half of the expected 4.5 per cent GDP growth — of a struggling economy — is under threat of being lost and Pakistan faces the spectre of a descent into a deeper economic quagmire.

Within months of Cyclone Bhola, an ideology — Bengali nationalism — feeding off economic deprivation and post disaster hopelessness took half the country away. This time, a renegade religious ideology — feeding off the consequences of the present disaster — is drooling to take away the remainder. This must not be allowed to happen.

FINANCING DEVELOPMENT

May 2011

RECENTLY, the Planning Commission (PC) was handed a paltry Rs280bn for the annual development plan 2011-12. With fiscal space closing in year after year, the federal government's allocated spending on infrastructure and social services is now down to Rs1,500 per Pakistani.

With the list of development projects earlier sent by the ministries in hand, and less than a fortnight to go before the budget announcement, the PC got to work with a simple formula: 171 projects on which less than 30 per cent of the work had been completed were to be abandoned. However, projects nearing completion were to receive funding. Most of these development projects are for water storage and irrigation, hydropower and grid improvement. Of course, little in the way of new projects could be accommodated.

I haven't seen the list of the 171 projects to be abandoned or the list of those to receive funding. But I know that with a bit of imagination and commercial savvy, a good number of projects in both lists can be structured for private investment, in modes such as BOT (Build-Operate-Transfer) or one of its many variants. That would greatly reduce the public-funding component of each project. What it would take is the detailed design and PC1 for a project — like a toll road — being converted to an investor-grade feasibility study and for a bankable concession agreement prepared by experienced legal experts.

Such a finished product can then be pitched to investors through what investment bankers refer to as 'transaction advisory'.

This involves investor road shows in financial capitals to generate investor interest, followed by procuring a winning bidder through a transparent international tendering process. Consulting, legal and transaction advisory services can be purchased for a fee typically amounting to two and a half per cent of the project cost plus a small retainer.

The head of an international development agency recently asked my view for the best way in which Pakistan could be assisted. "Just finance the retainer and success fee," was my response. "This way, your couple of million dollars would help us raise $100m in project funding from private sponsors, capital markets as well as from hedge funds, eximbanks and sovereign wealth funds." However, it's no good making an approach to these institutions without proper homework and unless project documentation of a very high standard has been prepared.

All this would mean a lot of work by the originating line ministries. At this time each year, clerks in these ministries populate a pro forma with topline project information updating last year's figures and making any required clerical adjustments in the form of adding and deleting from the list of projects. Instead of simply signing the dotted line at the bottom of this spreadsheet, senior bureaucrats would now have to spend time and intellectual effort to understand the projects in depth and then classify these into three groups: those that are commercially feasible in private mode, those that are marginally feasible and the remaining i.e. that are unfeasible in commercial mode.

Next, they would have to take the ones in the first category, then perhaps unbundle monolithic service models, identify where the revenue streams can be created and guide them through the above investor-feasibility process. The second category would be more difficult and require the ministries to calculate the viability gap which refers to the amount of subsidy the government will plug into the project's revenue stream each year until it is financially viable for the investor. In fact, multilateral lenders could be more responsive if approached to finance the viability gap, as opposed to funding an entire project. Once they are given bankable project documents and en-cashable government guarantees, private sponsors can easily mobilise financial commitments and bring the project to the next stage referred to as 'financial close'.

It is time to think outside the box. Instead, the ministries appear to have chosen the easy path of least resistance and parked all projects at the door of the PC requesting public funding, of which there is very little. So little in fact that at the present rate of accumulated 'throw forward', which refers to the nearly $150bn infrastructure projects awaiting funding, we have muddled into a 27-year-long tunnel just to clear the present backlog and during this time no additional project can be initiated.

Conversely, Rs280bn, together with savvy financial structuring and matched with private money, can arguably be leveraged into Rs1tr. This can begin wiping out the 'throw forward'. Repeated year after year, the timeline to clear the backlog of current projects can be reduced from 27 years to perhaps 12 which lands us in 2023, in an alternate future — a country with world-class transportation and civic infrastructure, cheaper energy from indigenous sources, a completed Diamer-Bhasha and all its children in school.

As a first step, instead of putting up the list to the PM, it may be best if the PC were to refer it back to the line ministries asking that from this year and every year following as many projects be identified, then structured for private investment and only then submitted to the PC for minimal public component. If they look around, one of the world's best legislative and institutional framework for public private partnership has been given to them already. The provinces with their Rs433bn should follow suit.

THE OTHER PAKISTAN

April 2011

GLORIOUS countryside lies between Rahim Yar Khan and Bahawalpur. Travelling across six districts in Punjab, before a blazing summer sets in, I experienced endless fields of wheat waiting to turn golden, of freshly harvested mustard, acres of ripe sugarcane and sprawling mango orchards.

Far from the drudge and gloom of metropolitan Pakistan, economic privation, traffic snarls, extreme religion and the cricket World Cup agony, this is another Pakistan. Over a quarter of a century after the green revolution ended the rural economy is back in boom, this time on the back of rising prices. The feel-good factor is all around.

Burgeoning commodity prices are churning unprecedented amounts of cash through the farm sector. I pass tractor-pulled trolleys laden with sugarcane waiting outside sugar mills. The crushing season is in full swing. Meanwhile, the flour mills are still grinding away at last year's surplus crop. This is an agro economy at serious work.

Alongside the cash economy, the place is also brimming with ideas, and with an entrepreneurial spirit. A young man I meet at Rahim Yar Khan's chamber of commerce has an IT degree and owns an ice cream distribution business spawning an elaborate cold chain across three districts. He tells me that sales are surging because rural society is transitioning to modern desserts which are now more affordable than traditional sweets like mithai and khoya.

Meanwhile, he's toying with the bigger vision of an electronic marketplace for agricultural produce. Live connectivity to grain mandis and markets for fresh produce and milk will empower farmers to obtain prices online and through their cellphones. He wants to materialise this and wants tips. I give him my two cents worth: study similar models, write a concept paper, galvanise partners around it, put in seed money and get the venture to mezzanine level.

For now the agricultural economy is growing more in value than in volume. As it does, it pulls in a rising demand for inputs. Fertiliser and agrochemical companies, some listed on the stock exchange are making record profits. Still, few find time to complain about rising input prices. With a population of 400,000, Rahim Yar Khan sports showrooms displaying cars, motorcycles and generators, fast food outlets and even private healthcare clinics.

Even then, not all the cash would appear to go into consumption. Pakistan now ranks amongst the world's top 10 markets for tractors. Alongside, and despite constrained credit to agriculture, farmers are investing in agricultural implements, irrigation channels and farm modernisation.

In 2008, the cotton harvest was in crisis. Ginning factories had no power and could not operate. There were sellers, mostly small farmers but there were no takers. Un-ginned cotton is a perishable commodity and the farmers were receiving throwaway prices. "How have you overcome that problem?" I asked my host, a local businessman, the owner of a number of cotton-ginning factories, as he treated us to a lavish lunch.

"Simple", he explains, "this year the ginners got together with the local utility company, Mepco. We've instituted a system whereby instead of intermittent hours of loadshedding we get it in one block of 12 hours. This way we can run the factory on one shift per day". With that problem behind him he now wanted to move on; that is, to a pasteurised milk business.

As the green revolution tapered off, a poultry revolution began; in the late 1970s. Ever since, Pakistan has been gnawing away at broiler chicken and there's no turning back. Today a dairy revolution is sweeping Pakistan. As the world's fifth largest milk producer, the country can only process three per cent of its milk production. Sitting in his factory office in Khanpur — one could have been in any plush office in a metropolis — we open his wireless notebook and download a pre-feasibility study for a milk pasteurising business from Smeda's website. We glean through it, and at a Rs160m capital outlay it looks doable for him.

The 'go' decision is made on the spot and my host asks me to recommend a good consultant.

In 2009, an NGO distributed young cattle on micro-credit to 1,000 small farmers and built an apex organisation to collect and market milk from these grass-roots. The Dutch consultant for the NGO informs me that a modern farmers' cooperative model is now evolving. Such models have long been in vogue in Europe and indeed in several developing countries. Usually the extended supply chain ends at farmer-owned retail outlets — co-ops. Why hasn't this concept gained traction in Pakistan?

Several of us seated around the conference table are unable to provide an intelligent answer until one of the NGO's employee's mutters something about biradari-based rivalries as the stumbling block. Indeed. After he hanged Bhutto, Ziaul Haq, to keep the PPP out of Punjab, had gone on to fragment politics in this province along biradari lines.

As I take off from Bahawalpur and four minutes into flight time, I look down to the spot where his C-130 must have come down. A glistening water channel is visible in the Sutlej over Khairpur Tamewali. This was a dry riverbed for the last several years. Until a year ago, water stress being brought on by rapidly depleting groundwater was a major concern. Now the aquifers have been recharged and as a post flood bonus from nature, soil deposition from floodwaters has enhanced yields.

And so Pakistan prepares to harvest another bumper wheat crop in 2011.

DON'T PAINT US BLACK

November 2011

WHEN two years ago I suggested a lucrative project investment opportunity to a Middle Eastern based investment banker friend, quite predictably his response was "heck, no its Pakistan's credit rating".

What then is a rating? In the words of the rating agencies themselves, it's an "informed opinion". So last week I asked my research associate to dig up the sources of information on which the rating agencies would typically base their opinion. She dug up a sample of ten leading international business and financial publications and extracted and analysed the last five years coverage on Pakistan. The same old predictable themes, phrases and thought patterns recurred: Osama bin Laden, safe havens, drone strikes, Taliban, energy crisis, floods, IMF, suicide bomb, nuclear weapons, terror attack, blasphemy and the occasional cricket.

Meanwhile, scores of foreign investors, businessmen and dignitaries who had visited our offices in the previous year were pleasantly surprised at Lahore's flamboyant, lush and hospitable environment something quite in contrast to what the media in their home countries had told them. And yet, two years after my banker friend brushed aside the Pakistan opportunity, it was not Pakistan with its B negative credit rating that was brushing against default. Instead the house was coming down on economies like Greece, Portugal, Italy, Spain, Ireland and the recent "almost default" of the US. Pakistan on the other hand has gained territory with its current account deficit turning to surplus and its foreign exchange reserves climbing to an all time high.

The Pakistan discourse appears to have gotten caught in a closed loop and vicious "copy paste cycle". It has come to be dominated by media coverage, broker reports and rating agencies that feed off each other and betray a lack of both, original thinking and an understanding of the fundamentals. Three quarters of Pakistan's urban workforce finds work in the informal sector. Almost half of the rural agricultural workforce is engaged in subsistence agriculture. Together these constitute the bedrock underneath Pakistan's economy – below which it can't sink – and essentially that is where it sits today. At worst this is an underpinning that limits systemic risk in the "Pakistan System". At best it's a launch pad.

Cliché is a French term for a stereotype printing block which produces the same page over and over again. One way to break this printing block is to dwell on two notions. The first is Certain Realities about Pakistan's present i.e. that which is known and hard to disagree with. The second is the notion of Real Certainties about its future i.e., that which is plausible and hard to dismiss.

Let's turn to some certain realities: As the Arab Spring turns to summer, it remains to be seen which way the cookie will crumble, and once it does, how the individual states fare with their decades long course to democracy. Pakistan has already settled its questions in its constitutional framework of 1973 and today there are few here who would question the constitution and challenge the state – and I will address the Taliban in a moment. With a vibrant multiparty system and the peculiar but familiar South Asian brand of democracy, there is broad agreement by all parties and the military on maintaining a liberal and investment friendly regime and on private sector led growth. But beyond that, Pakistan's political system is beginning to demonstrate a remarkable propensity to resolve some of the most contentious political issues. Some worth mentioning are the devolution of power to the provinces, the need or otherwise for more provinces, the mode of governance at the district and local levels, water sharing, allocation of funds and fighting the war on terror. On indicators such as freedom of press, independence of judiciary and on the relative ease of doing business, Pakistan already punches above its weight

A large indigenous market, a young and upwardly mobile population as well as a large and affluent overseas diaspora are certain realities. Pakistan's underutilized position as the fastest transit corridor offering the closest seaport access for the rapidly developing Xingiang province of Western China and for Afghanistan's over USD 1 trillion mineral wealth is a certain reality. Pakistan's position as a sleeping giant in the US $ 600 billion market for halal food products is yet another certain reality.

Perhaps the rating agencies and media ought to also probe into the country's best in class legislation and regulatory frameworks covering private power production, telecom, banking, stock exchanges and for public private partnership. In an attempt to create economic stimulus central banks in Japan, the US and Europe have gradually dropped interest rates to near zero. Pakistan's present high 13 percent interbank rate signifies tremendous reserve energy to create that stimulus when the time comes.

The future of most economies may now be uncertain. Nevertheless, there are some real certainties about Pakistan's future that are plausible and hard to dismiss. The Taliban is on the run. Its vigilantism has been militarily defeated. The eventual defeat of its ideology is a real certainty. Improving relations with India and the emergence of a South Asian regional economic integration is also a real certainty. Also, once the lawmakers are ready to bring the untaxed sectors into the tax net, the doubling of the country's present 9 percent tax to GDP ratio is also a certainty. The consequent retirement of Pakistan's entire public debt in a few years of this happening is also a certainty.

Driven by robust corporate earnings year after year the KSE 100 index has outperformed its peers and indeed the MSCI Bric and every single OECD index. And now suddenly it's me who doesn't have the heart to tell my banker friend that ratings or no ratings, had he invested in the KSE 100 in January 2009, he'd have doubled his wealth by now. Money talks after all and everything else, including copy pasting negative clichés, walks.

BETWEEN BUDGET AND ELECTIONS

June 2012

THE budget proposals presented a week ago together with the Annual Plan lack a sense of realism as well as action plans on how economic growth will be achieved.

The government's approach appears to be to throw money at key sectors — where the ministries and executing agencies, both in the centre and the provinces have a proven incapacity. Similarly, there appears to be no plan to halt the gradual downward drift of the rupee. This is like spelling out a hope and then praying for rain.

Let's get real. The present situation of governance in Pakistan is in a state of near paralysis. This is for three reasons: lack of political will, lack of fiscal space and the fact that real governance is in the hands of a civil service bureaucracy that runs on operating systems rooted in the 19th century which are unable to respond to the requirements of the 21st century. From this enormously handicapped position what would be a realistic economic 'to do' list for the ruling coalition for its remaining term — even if the sole objective is to deliver some results in time for the next elections? Let me stake out a path that involves working on only three or four big ticket items.

After four wasted years, reforming the civil service or the power sector are now best left to the new government which will be in office by mid 2013. In the meantime, by doing two things the ruling party and its allies can curtail the paralysing power outages within weeks. One, that every single installed megawatt of thermal capacity should be enabled, provided fuel and brought into operation. Two, adopt a zero tolerance policy towards power theft and a '30-day tolerant' policy on nonpayment beyond due date. As uninterrupted power is restored it can create, at the very least, $6m in value added each day — potentially adding one percentage point to GDP growth.

Energy shortages have also decimated our exports. Unfortunately, at this stage given little exportable surplus and the global environment, increasing exports appears unlikely in the short term. That should be put aside for the next government. Nevertheless, decreasing imports has the same effect on GDP growth in that every dollar of import reduced brings one dollar of growth in the economy. It also helps arrest the slide of the rupee.

Pakistan's imports in the present year are likely to cross $40bn. At $15bn, the single largest item is petroleum. Within petroleum, diesel and furnace oil constitute the lion's share of our requirement.

The number of trucks plying on highways is the second area generating colossal economic waste. If this freight is put on the rail system, I am informed by experts that this single action will cut the expense on high speed diesel by 30 per cent.

In the same stroke the government may allow diesel and furnace oil imports from India. Together these measures will lower the import bill, relieve stress on our foreign exchange reserves and add another percentage point to GDP growth.

Turning now to the big battle against shrinking fiscal space, and I'm afraid the government's bumbling is at its worst. There is even talk of approaching the IMF. Let's stay real. Given our recent track record with the IMF, the present euro debt crisis and Pakistan's state of relations with Nato, what will be IMF's most likely response to our overture? 'Go back, implement VAT and then we'll sit down for a chat.'

That buck is best passed to the next government. Pushed into the corner, the government will quickly come face to face with the most likely and the worst-case scenario: borrow from banks and indiscriminately print more money. Result: increasing inflation, rising unemployment and a plummeting rupee. Everyone will lose, particularly the underprivileged and the next government that will inherit the mess in 10 months time.

Is there an alternative path? When options are tight what else can you do? You look for low hanging fruit; for some quick wins.

Some time ago there was a list that was shuttling back and forth between the Prime Minister's Secretariat and the FBR offices on opposite sides of Constitution Avenue. Then all went quiet. On it were 776,000 identified prospects that own property, take multiple foreign trips abroad, own cars, have bank accounts but do not fulfil their income tax filing obligations. For too long they've enjoyed a free ride.

There is an estimated Rs450bn immediate potential here that can open up fiscal space and if crafted intelligently, can be a master political stroke by the ruling coalition to deliver in time for the next elections. Put to good use, the recovered money can help ease inflation, increase output, create jobs and bring about a reduction in discount rate — adding another percentage point to GDP growth.

Who knows, it may even prove to be the wave on which the ruling coalition can ride into the next election but for that it must start taking positions — and action — on the above issues before others bring them into the political arena. Taken together these few items could in a relatively short period raise our GDP growth rate to six or even seven per cent and perhaps position Pakistan, in these times of a global financial crunch, as an emerging market to be taken seriously by the international financial community.

At that stage, the reforms in civil service, power sector and value added tax can be unfolded, which become the second-post-electoral wave and send out a signal that better times are ahead.

A LACK OF CLARITY

December 2012

THE Chief of the National Accountability Bureau (NAB), has confused graft, theft and economic losses. By adding the three he's trying to add apples, oranges and monkeys.

It was bad enough for the NAB chief to release at a press conference a confused two-pager that is built on unsound reasoning. It was worse that none of the media persons present there could see through the eyewash.

When the former admiral says we're losing Rs13 billion each day to corruption then the perception that gets created in the mind of the ordinary citizen is that the government, which consists of ruling party politicians and state functionaries, is eating up Rs13bn of public money each day.

Clearly that is not the case, even in his report. Not even close. So what's wrong with what the admiral says and what's wrong with the 'position paper'?

In a nutshell? Everything.

Basically the argument goes that the tax-to-GDP ratio is nine per cent and can "be easily" enhanced to 18 per cent. Whilst the proposition may be true, the attribution of Rs7bn daily losses to tax evasion is misplaced. Above all, this is circular reasoning; simplistic and fallacious.

But before we get into that, let's stay clearheaded here and not mix up evasion with graft. When a wholesale trader chooses not to declare his actual turnover, and pockets the withholding tax money then that's stealing, or what we term as tax evasion. The taxman, mainly because he can become a nuisance for the wholesale trader, may receive a small percentage of the evaded amount and that is graft.

So of the supposed Rs7bn that escapes the tax net each year, how much finds its way into the hands of corrupt (public) officials? A small fraction, I would say — not even 10 per cent. Does that mean that the remaining 90 per cent finds itself in the pockets of dishonest citizens then? Even that may not be true given the extensive exemptions and tax-free statuses enjoyed by many sectors including agriculture.

Large sectors of the economy remain outside the tax net because of lack of documentation. The resulting cash economy is what creates a conducive environment for evasion.

To be fair, the present government attempted to introduce VAT, which is the basic instrument in documenting national economies and raising tax revenue. It was other political parties pandering to their urban constituencies that undermined its imposition.

From the media the swansong enters parliament and amidst the ensuing din and clamour, rational argument gets drowned. A coolheaded parliament would first have sought clarity — and simply asked the NAB chief a series of questions such as if he knew the difference between corruption, economic losses, electricity theft, land grabbing and other types of fraudulent activity.

Did he know the difference between holders of public office and private citizens? Did he know the difference between public accounts and private transactions? Instead of seeking out clarity, parliament has gone in the opposite direction; denials, counter-allegations and calls for apology from the media. More confusion, more clutter.

Next stop from parliament is the public meeting — where Imran Khan, true to his style, is at the forefront of sowing more confusion in the public mind as he attempts to link the NAB report to "70 per cent of PML-N politicians" who he labels as tax dodgers.

Good chance that they are tax dodgers, but Khan's sophistry here is so complex that unbundling it will need either another column or a cross-questioning session.

On to more foolishness now — two days after its release the NAB spokesman "clarifies" and holds the Punjab government responsible for 65 per cent of the graft.

Ah, but wait a minute Mr Spokesman. Didn't your report attribute Rs7bn of the total Rs13bn daily losses to tax evasion? And isn't the FBR responsible for tax collection and evasion? Is the FBR under the Punjab government?

Or by corruption do you also mean to include non-imposition of agriculture tax by the Punjab government. Aren't we getting unusually creative here with definitions?

Also included in the corruption are totally unrelated sums such as power losses, including losses due to loadshedding, losses incurred (indeed profits foregone) of the state-owned enterprises, cost overruns in implementation of mega projects. None of these belong in the corruption category but appear to have been included to inflate the figure.

What would it take to undo this damage? Basically the NAB chief should go, and the author(s) of the 'position paper' be brought forward to answer technical questions by a panel of neutral experts, who can then give their position on the 'position paper'.

Secondly, the Institute of Chartered Accountants of Pakistan should step up to the media — or vice versa — and help dissect the numbers and clear the confusion. So should Transparency International — just to set the record straight. What is corruption, what is theft and what economic loss means.

Lastly, as with most other issues in this country, there is need to build consensus around defining corruption and recognising that all forms of evil are not corruption which refers to receiving graft payments by holders of public office (upwards from the patwari).

Once the target has been defined in this precise a manner, you can ready, aim and fire. The terms of reference for the new accountability commission which will replace NAB ought to be very focused with defined performance indicators on what is required of it.

As with the war against terrorism, the Kalabagh dam, the blasphemy law and so much else, without a clear recognition of any issue, without unbundling its complexity, you can never solve it, you only confound it further.

POLICY BEFORE TRANSPORT

February 2013

THE Punjab government says that the metro bus project has been completed at a cost of nearly Rs30 billion. By the time all the invoices are in, the final figure may well be considerably higher.

What is not being mentioned is the provincial budget that only had an allocation of Rs11bn for this project.

Nevertheless the Rs19bn cost overrun is a mundane issue and is not the reason why I'm writing. On the other hand I do get alarmed when I don't hear quality discussions on important issues of public policy. First let's look at some context.

The metro bus project is actually a much watered down version of what was to be the Phase 1 (green line) of the Light Rail Mass Transit System (LRMTS), an elevated monorail. Its subsequent phases were going to include the blue, purple and orange lines. On a city level, this would have been a strategic project giving Lahore a system comparable to the Delhi Metro.

In 2008, the Asian Development Bank agreed to provide a technical assistance loan and help the Punjab government develop the LRMTS and find an investor/operator consortium. A few months later, in a memo to his board in June 2008 the CEO of ADB reported that no investment bank appeared to be interested in the job.

Investment bankers had two major reservations with regard to the LRMTS. One, given its poor writ, they doubted that the Punjab government would be able to acquire the land smoothly and in a timely fashion for the transit corridor. Two, given the Punjab government's credit rating they doubted it would be able to furnish a credible traffic guarantee.

Far from addressing the concerns of investors, the incoming PML-N government did not even appear enthusiastic about LRMTS, perhaps holding the misguided view that this was Pervaiz Elahi's project. The Punjab bureaucracy also allowed the project files to slide to the bottom of the pile and the subject was never brought up in meetings. In due course,

ADB's offer lapsed.

Even after that, there were consortia from Malaysia and China that showed interest in the project. Given the PML-N's tense working relationship with the ruling coalition in Islamabad, senior bureaucrats in Lahore could foresee the slog and stumbles ahead in terms of arranging financial guarantees for the project. On its part the PML-N also felt that the LRMTS was going to be a long haul whilst it was looking for ribbons to cut before elections in 2013.

Shunning the hard work, the Punjab government decided to go for the lazy option. Buses would run in designated corridors on existing roads. Worse still, it published the RFP (Request for Proposals) for this project inviting private-sector investors without conducting a proper feasibility study.

The investors who did respond and carried out some due diligence complained about the poor quality of information. For example the extent of the minimum revenue guarantee was not mentioned and something basic like a toll sensitivity analysis was not done.

The information was vague, generic and insufficient to draft a concession agreement or to base an investment decision on. Two bumbling bureaucratic years later, the last of the prospective investors walked away.

What do you do after you flunk the midterm? You go back, crunch your numbers, prepare better-quality project documents then re-invite bids. Instead the Punjab government once again chose a short cut and decided to venture where the angels had feared to tread. It would throw its own money at the project.

Spending money is easy. In fact, it would throw half of the province's infrastructure development budget of Rs63bn into one corridor in one city.

This brings us to the questions of public policy that we are not hearing.

The State Bank estimates that $150bn is required to fund the hundreds of infrastructure projects that are awaiting development in Pakistan. Even if we conservatively assume one-third of these to be in Punjab then, with the province's infrastructure budget of less than $630 million per year, it will take 79 years just to cover this backlog.

Should the government be funding these projects or should it play the enabler and let the private sector take the lead? Is there a public private partnership framework and legislation in the country? What is its purpose and when will we start to see private money flow into infrastructure projects?

Should the government be in the business of running buses? What have we learnt from our previous experience of government running buses in this country? Is the government doing a good job of running the railways, PIA and the Pakistan National Shipping Corporation? What will be different this time round?

What is the plan going forward, one year, three years and 10 years from today? If the government could not attract investors on the BOT (build operate transfer) model then how will it attract investors on the privatisation model?

Is this an investment that will create future national wealth? In the 1990s there were voices imploring Sharif to invest the $1bn being poured into the M2 motorway into upgrading and modernising the railways instead. Is it reasonable to expect that a dollar invested in 1997 ought to have brought back $20 to the national economy today?

Warren Buffet could probably be considered the 20th century's most successful investor. Had he been asked in the 1990s for advice on where he thought Pakistan should invest this money, might he have suggested a state of the art hydrocracker plant because it would spawn the development of a globally competitive chemical industry in Pakistan?

But those choices are for the people of Pakistan to make and as we do that it would be useful if we are exposed to better quality analysis and more informed discussion on matters of public policy. That is something I find missing from the national discourse today.

THE ROAD TO PRIVATIZATION

May 2013

AN economic turnaround can be brought about by unlocking value from assets that are presently under-performing.

Basically, to instigate economic growth would require a jump in the output of goods and services that the economy produces. That impetus can come from the privatisation of the 200 or so state-owned enterprises (SOEs).

Whilst the exact amount of losses being incurred by these enterprises would depend on what you count and how you count, the final figure would probably be in the ballpark of the annual defence budget. Even then, this is the smaller issue. The larger one being the opportunity cost of not taking action, a theme we will return to in a moment.

When approaching an acquisition, financiers and businesspeople are looking more at its cash flow potential and less at its assets (land, buildings, and machinery). We gain a better perspective by viewing these SOEs (businesses) as going concerns rather than as a garage sale of assets.

Often these assets have greater countervailing liabilities leaving many of our SOEs with negative net worth. To ensure a smooth privatisation journey, the government's policy planners would do well to explain these differentiations to the general public, the media and to the legal fraternity.

The infamous Steel Mills case of 2006 ran into snags when it was felt that the price being offered was less than the cost of the land. This could have been avoided if the deal had been structured for the going concern. Nevertheless the Pakistan Steel judgment does bring some lessons on the need to improve transparency and to ensure that a level playing field is maintained at all times.

Sprawling units like Pakistan Steel and Pakistan Railways (after restructuring and corporatisation) can be offered on the basis of leasehold land (granting temporary and conditional rights on the land) instead of freehold (which grants property rights in perpetuity).

For the investor, this would bring down the capital outlay while the government would retain title to all its properties. In a going concern the real value is created from satisfied customers, improved business performance and increased cash flows. From the point of view of efficient business operations, it matters little whether the land underneath is leased or owned.

It would be advisable to offer additional incentives to privatised businesses that also undertake to list on the stock market. Apart from broad basing ownership this would increase the size, and arguably the depth, of our capital markets. At present, 23 majority state-owned enterprises — led by the OGDC, the national oil and gas company — account for over a third of the total market capitalisation of the Karachi Stock Exchange.

It is also critical to have a pro-privatisation management in the entity being sold. Nothing can be more discouraging than for a bidder to meet the management of the company only to be told what a bad decision it would be to buy the asset.

An unwilling management can also stall the process by not providing the correct data or withholding data until the last moment. In worst cases it can incite employees to demonstrate against the sale — and you have all the ingredients of a failed transaction. Taking management and employees along not only smoothes the process, it is also the fair way to proceed. Another key determinant of success is the visible commitment on part of the government. The National Power Construction Company has been taken to the bidding stage on a number of occasions, by a number of governments. Then the process has been abandoned. This has left bidders completely disillusioned (having spent thousands of dollars in due diligence) and now they refuse to take the process seriously.

The moral of the story is that when the decision to sell has been taken, then market forces should be allowed to take over. Investors are astute people and if the government ensures full disclosure and a fair and competitive bidding process, they will arrive at a fair market-based price. Once you approve the successful bidder, the transfer process should be mechanical.

On a priority, the government must undertake the long delayed policy reforms — particularly in the energy sector — and other sectoral and regulatory strengthening centred on key entities being privatised. In tandem it should launch a communication programme to explain the merits of the privatisation and reform agenda to the public.

According to a recent report in the Telegraph, 100 shares of British

Gas bought during its privatisation in 1986 for £135 would today be worth £1,682. Compared to the FTSE 100 which has trebled over the same time period, British Gas has increased 12 times. These forgone profits represent the opportunity cost of not taking action — which we had alluded to earlier.

Pakistan too has a reasonably good track record of privatisation. Since 1991, 167 entities — banks, energy companies, telecom operators, fertiliser plants, ghee mills, cement factories, automotive plants, chemical and light engineering industries — have been privatised to yield $9 billion to the exchequer. Most of the entities have fared well under private management and their share price valuations have contributed to creating national wealth.

In several of these, notably KAPCO and PTCL, the government retains its majority shareholding and earns dividends on their profits. In many of these entities, private owners have injected technology and management practices and enhanced these government assets to blue chip grade.

Lastly they continue to pay taxes at the corporate income tax rate of 35pc. The path to prosperity has seldom been more visible, illuminated as it is on both sides.

This piece was co-authoured with Umar Shereef, Senior Partner at Haidermota & Co, Barristers at Law & Corporate counselors, and who has advised on over 25 successful privatisations.

RESTRUCTURING PIA

June 2013

PAKISTAN'S national airline lost Rs33 billion last year. This is more than what a fully loaded Boeing 777 would cost.

Few who know the airline business would have expected PIA to make a profit last year. Since the start of the financial crisis in 2008 the global airline industry has been hit by a double whammy.

It has seen a cut in business travel and a drop in leisure travel. On the other hand, high crude oil prices have squeezed yields.

That said; one cannot let PIA off the hook. This is for two reasons. First it has not adequately taken advantage of market opportunities available to it and second, it has let its costs creep well beyond global industry benchmarks.

On the market opportunities front, we have a significant Pakistani diaspora in North America and in Europe. This represents an alluring, captive market that would be the envy of any legacy national carrier. Western airlines typically do not fly to Pakistan.

All PIA has to do is operate direct flights from North American and European cities into major Pakistani cities offering the proposition "fastest way to get you there". The two main ingredients of this proposition would be affordable fares and on-time performance.

Sadly though, PIA has conceded two thirds of this market to other (mostly Gulf-based) carriers. Financially, this corresponds to Rs60bn in annual revenue that PIA's competitors have taken away.

Even if half of this can be won back over three years then the airline is looking at a 9pc annual growth rate at a time when most other airlines are stagnant. And this is just on the back of business regained in one segment: the Western hemisphere.

Now to be fair to PIA, the Gulf airlines (and airports) are driven by more than commercial considerations. They are in fact strategic play pieces, part of a larger vision to position these countries as world destinations and to build their image and global profile. This is not unlike the motivation for which countries host the Olympic Games.

It can be argued therefore that PIA is often up against competition of a variety that goes beyond the commercial and profit motive. Still it must cherry pick, then focus on and build its star routes, anchored in the proposition "fastest way to get you there".

In these markets, traditional marketing has given way to search engine marketing, using which customers search flights, obtain fares and compare routings and timings.

Digital media has opened up new customer touch points which include price comparison websites and social media. It is not uncommon, for example, for customers to be engaging with the airline on Twitter — in real time — discussing meal options on a specific flight.

In addition most airlines have launched their own mobile apps allowing their customers to book tickets, to check-in and to manage their frequent flier accounts from their mobile phones.

Similarly, the domestic market from which PIA derives half its revenue is clearly underserved. The domestic travellers seek convenient flight times and on-time performance. Then there is a segment seeking budget fares.

Service propositions can be developed around these needs and have existed in the past. And while the global airline industry may be facing overcapacity, for PIA there is latent demand in the domestic sector offering several years of growth opportunity. The other main segments are outbound travel from Pakistan for business and for leisure. Here the in-flight experience and holiday airfares are important ingredients of the customer proposition. Then there is the religious travel segment and finally the expatriate Pakistanis in the Gulf region who are time poor and baggage heavy.

It doesn't make sense to increase market share when each flight is losing you money.

This brings us to the second issue: costs creeping beyond industry benchmarks.

While much is made of overstaffing, in fact PIA's cost inefficiencies are in its fleet, that last year guzzled Rs61bn worth of fuel. This represents 55pc of total revenue. In terms of the global airline industry, fuel makes up 35pc of total costs.

Meanwhile Australia's Qantas — perhaps because of carbon tax considerations — keeps it as low as 28pc. PIA's 55pc is therefore hard to accept.

In addition PIA's load factor at 70pc is below par. Lastly, the fleet downtime is high with aircraft kept on the ground for want of spares or payment for fuel.

From the perspective of a strategic operating plan, an airline's business analysis does not begin with aircraft but with the market forecast. However, once the traffic estimates are ascertained, then the most optimal aircraft solutions are found.

If it turns out that the aircraft available from within the airline's fleet are a poor fit with requirements then a fleet restructuring may become necessary. Alternately it may become necessary for reasons of fuel efficiency or aircraft obsolescence.

If this turns out to be the case then the management and the airline board would need to be given a free hand to take the necessary decisions without outside meddling or interference.

They must also be allowed to choose between buying and leasing the aircraft and to evaluate and decide on the most viable financing plan. Needless to say, a onetime bailout may be extended against a sound business plan so that the airline is recapitalised and these ratios can be fixed.

The other 45pc of the expenses are non-fuel expenses. Whilst drastic reductions in manpower expenses may be unrealistic, airlines around the world have taken fiscal cost control measures which have included contract renegotiations, process improvements and restructuring agent commissions. But if over half of my expense is fuel, then half the time of my management looking for cost savings should be spent here.

JACKPOT BOOMTOWNS

September 2013

MELBOURNE'S reputation as the world's most liveable city is well deserved. I spent most of last year there. As well as a chic city centre and immaculate suburbs, there's non-stop annual activity featuring events like the Australian Open grand slam tennis, the Formula 1 Australian grand prix, a Derby horserace, an international film festival, a food and wine festival and a hectic calendar of sport, cultural and entertainment activity.

Riverboats ply up and down the Yarra River, which is Melbourne's answer to the Thames in London or the Seine in Paris. The city's central business district is to the one side of the river. On the other side, the Southbank promenade, sprawls the Crown casino and entertainment complex, the largest in the southern hemisphere.

Australians are avid gamblers and gambling is a well-regulated industry. Licensed operators clock in $20 billion in revenues, paying $5bn in taxes every year. Meanwhile the Australian productivity commission calculates the benefits derived by the 70pc of Australians who gamble (if joy could be measured and quantified as a dollar amount), to significantly outweigh the costs, which mostly relate to the problem gamblers.

It contends that the costs can be further reduced through improved regulatory measures. But while Australia ranks as one of the world's happiest societies, Australians are not night owls, most preferring to turn in early.

Emerging Asia on the other hand is another story. "A little gambling is good for health," goes an old Chinese maxim, "but too much can drive you mad." So it was on Chinese New Year in 2010 that Singapore opened the Resorts World Sentosa, a casino complex that also integrates a Universal Studios theme park as well as hotels and a convention centre.

Shortly afterwards, another such integrated resort followed; the Marina Bay Sands. The $10bn in foreign direct investment have quite arguably kept the effects of the global financial crisis from engulfing Singapore. The resorts charge a $100 entry fee which goes towards covering "social costs", a euphemism for issues concerning problem gamblers.

In adjoining Malaysia, Mahathir Mohammed had promoted the development of integrated gaming and entertainment resorts in the scenic Genting highlands. The drive up there from Kuala Lumpur is not unlike that to Bhurban from Islamabad. The Genting group is the Malaysian conglomerate that led the development. Today its market capitalisation stands at around $50bn.

Driven by supercharged economic performance over recent decades, China has churned out millionaires and billionaires in ever increasing numbers. They're always up for a bit of travel that involves the thrill of new gambling destinations. Not surprisingly, the Pacific Rim has edged out Western hot spots such as Las Vegas, Atlantic City and Monte Carlo.

The Economist reports that the Philippines is developing four impressive casino complexes on a chunk of reclaimed land overlooking Manila Bay. It also reports that in Japan, a move is afoot for parliament to introduce legislation to liberalise gambling.

Other than ethnic and sectarian strife and target killings, Karachi and Beirut may have few similarities today. But in the early 1970s, both cities could boast almost idyllic peace and safety as also their nightlife, cabaret clubs and bars. Western expats were a common sight, whether visiting or working in Karachi's corporate and educational sectors.

Back then, Karachi and Beirut may well have been regarded as culture cousins in almost a sort of rivalry that would position them as alternative destinations.

Driving 22km along the scenic coast road north of Beirut, one comes to the Casino du Liban; set on a cliff, overlooking the Mediterranean. Its architect was the one who later designed the Clifton Beach Casino that was taking shape in Karachi in the mid 1970s.

Steve Inskeep, in his book Instant City: Life and Death in Karachi recounts his conversation with Tufail (Tony) Shaikh, sponsor of the project. "We knew there was trouble in Beirut. We knew we would get all the Arabs here" he quotes Shaikh as telling him. At that time, the oil shock of 1974 was rapidly creating thousands of Gulf Arab millionaires.

The regulations for the Clifton Beach Casino were to allow foreigners only; but Pakistanis who paid high income taxes could also come. Inskeep also tells us that to run the casino, Shaikh had arranged to bring in Stanley Ho, one of the world's richest men who owned extensive concessions for gambling in Macau. "People who don't want to gamble, they can come and watch the floor show, have dinner, enjoy the evening. People who want to gamble, they can gamble," Shaikh explained.

In 1976 Lebanon slipped into civil war and a window of opportunity briefly opened for Karachi. Then, just before the final approval for the grand opening, in May 1977, the curtain fell. Bhutto's government, under pressure from Islamists, declared Friday as the weekly holiday and banned gambling. The appeasement didn't work and within two months Ziaul Haq took over and the window slammed shut. Today not just Gulf Arabs but all foreigners including most foreign airlines shun Pakistan.

And what happened to Stanley Ho? The Economist reports that by 2002 he was holding a monopoly on gambling in Macau. Last year, Macau's turnover totalled six times Las Vegas. China's economic miracle has fuelled spectacular growth and each day droves of well-to-do Chinese board the high-speed train to Macau which is now also being linked overland with Hong Kong's huge airport.

Meanwhile, his son had reached a deal with Russian authorities to open a casino in Vladivostok, Russia's Far East which is closer to Beijing than to Moscow. The world keeps moving and its work goes on.

FAR BEHIND IN THE RACE

December 2013

WHEN the rupee started to weaken earlier this year, the government responded by intervening in the currency markets.

Speculators knew that the government with limited reserves could not play the game for long. That is when the State Bank pulled the second lever; it began to raise interest rates.

When there was no let up in the capital flight the government put a lid on the amount of cash that could be taken out. But still the rupee continued to slide so the government decided to approach the UAE government for the remaining $800 million proceeds from the PTCL privatisation to build reserves.

Then recently it offered twin amnesties to black money and to tax evaders. The naive hope is that this money — instead of being 'dollarised' — will be invested in manufacturing ventures.

Managing exchange rates is a firefighting measure. At best you deal with symptoms of the real malaise and delay the inevitable. At a fundamental level, Pakistan's economic competitiveness has been in steady decline over the years.

Today the country ranks 133rd out of 148 surveyed. This means that most goods are now not viable for production in Pakistan and the few that are, are fast losing their shine. This applies to not just manufactured goods but many of our farm products as well.

In a free trade world, this situation places Pakistan at a major disadvantage. A free trade agreement with China has brought an influx of Chinese goods but very little has gone in the opposite direction. Going forward, the situation for Pakistan looks set to worsen.

Two factors have brought us to this pass. One is the failure to develop indigenous energy resources. Today a substantial part of our import bill is fuel. The second and far more serious has been our failure to develop efficient, world beating industries in some key sectors (with few exceptions like cement, fertiliser and textile spinning).

The path taken by Japan and other high-performing Asian 'Tiger' economies, all of which were energy deficient, required them to first accumulate capital, then deploy that capital efficiently in a few sectors and finally pursue rapid technological catch-up with the West.

This was done on the back of a high standard of national education and a high domestic savings rate. In Pakistan these factors were not present.

A third ingredient was central planning, which in laissez faire capitalist economies plays a limited but vital role. Once a national economic vision is spelt out, the Five Year Plan is the instrument that helps direct scarce economic resources and necessary interventions supported with enabling policies towards sectors that have to be built.

In our case, the Five Year Plans were of academic value and even that process was later all but abdicated.

Usually a developing economy would build its industrial backbone on the basis of two primary investments. A steel mill that would help kick-start a downstream engineering industry, and a hydrocracker that would make available petrochemical feedstock and spawn the development of a chemical industry. This could be thought of as the hardware.

The national innovative capacity is the ability of a country to produce and commercialise a flow of innovative technology over the long term. This can be thought of as the software.

Empirical studies have found that innovative capacities of economies are very closely correlated with both competitiveness and with GDP.

Pakistan's steel mill never really got going and the hydrocracker plant never progressed beyond the feasibility study phase. No government bothered to develop or even articulate a credible innovation strategy.

Research and academic institutions remained weak and under-resourced with little linkage to industry. Pakistani firms also do not spend much on R&D, preferring instead to buy licensed technologies or turnkey industrial solutions.

So at this stage can anything be done? The difficulty is that after decades of inaction and decay we are left with very little strategic space to work with. The upside is that Pakistan's large domestic market still makes this an attractive place to do business.

To start, one needs to ask the question: which three or four industrial sectors can we become world leaders in? This is a contentious exercise because it will also identify certain sectors that may not receive much economic resources. This is because large-scale resources will need to be diverted towards the selected sectors.

Any strategic process creates winners and losers. Big push export strategies would need to be implemented in these three or four industrial sectors in addition to the large domestic market so the necessary scale effects can be achieved. With this in mind, a series of interventions will need to be planned.

The other and somewhat less daunting challenge would be to develop indigenous energy resources.

A politically neutral approach that tries to give everything to everyone would be disingenuous. All that will produce is a patchwork of non-strategic policies often at cross purposes with each other. These statutory regulatory orders or SROs as they are known promote a culture of crony capitalism and do not make for long-term policy stability.

As usual, the hardest part is the politics.

Selecting winners and losers, resisting pressure from vested interest when their privilege gets taken away, refusing to backtrack once a decision is made, preventing mission creep, ie saying 'NO' to pressure for inclusion of more and more sectors to the list, implementing the necessary reforms, bringing the full force of law to deal with violent religiously inspired groups that impose an economic cost on business activity and shatter confidence.

The commodity most needed is political will, and as of now, that is the commodity that is in short supply.

THE LAST CHANCE

June 2014

SOUTH Indian-style prawns cooked in spices and coconut milk next to a Lucknavi specialty, galouti kebabs and an array of mouth-watering dishes, signified a celebration of the cuisines of South Asia. And bringing the leadership of the Saarc countries together for his swearing-in was a skilful manoeuvre from Indian Prime Minister Narendra Modi. It signified a celebration of South Asian democracy; all eight Saarc leaders are democratically elected.

The last time India and Europe stood at similar stages of historical development was in the 16th century. As Mughal Emperor Akbar expanded his empire across North India, Europe was experiencing plague deaths as well as terrible massacres and conquests. But at another level, a renaissance of learning and ideas was spreading fast across the continent. Thus began the rise of the Western civilisation. Thereafter, their paths diverged.

Today, South Asia faces the monumental challenge of meeting the basic need of its inhabitants for food, water, energy, healthcare, education and access to justice. In its essence the agenda facing all Saarc countries is the twin challenge of human development and economic betterment of its people: How to get incomes to rise, how to raise revenues for the state, how to build quality institutions and government capacity that can address this agenda.

In 1980, China's per capita income stood at $300, in line with Saarc countries. Deng Xiaoping's reforms had only just begun, premised as they were on de-collectivisation of agriculture, opening up to foreign direct investment and enforcement of a one-child policy.

These measures were followed up by privatisation and allowing private enterprise. Today China's demographic dividend may be running out, but the average Chinese enjoys a per capita income nearly five times that of their South Asian counterpart.

So where next for South Asia? Demographers and development

specialists may differ whether South Asia's demographic dividend would last another two decades or four. At any rate, without jobs this dividend becomes a liability. But these decades may represent South Asia's last chance.

Modi's challenges are domestic — slowing growth, rising inflation, an economy that is not creating enough jobs and where government finances are a mess. The expectations from him are huge, as is his burden of responsibility. The fact that India is riddled with corruption and crony capitalism further complicates matters. Economic engagement with Pakistan is probably peripheral, if at all visible on his radar at this stage.

Can Modi deliver? After all, what he did in Gujarat, can it not be scaled up, replicated in the rest of India? Some regard this sceptically; a 'provincial' solution to a national problem. True, Modi made Gujarat India's most favoured investment destination and in 2013 Gujarat bagged nearly a quarter of the country's industrial investment proposals.

Most of that success can be put down to the favourable incentives Modi's Gujarat would offer to cut itself a larger slice of India's cake — and this is not the same thing as India getting a bigger cake.

A case in point would be Tata's decision to move the location of its automobile assembly plant for the Nano from West Bengal to Gujarat. From the left pocket to the right pocket. Similarly for FDI, once the decision to invest in India had been made in Tokyo, Seoul, London or Rotterdam the next step would be to select the site location. And Gujarat was where land acquisition was the fastest.

Granted, this may be a rather harsh evaluation of Modi's performance in Gujarat; still the question is, can the South Asian governments in power today (and their successors) deliver in the next couple of decades what has eluded their predecessors in the last six? After all Deng Xiaoping did it in China. But unlike the Communist Party whose party structure was organised from the ground up, from the village commune to the politburo, South Asian governments have to depend on decaying colonial-era state structures for implementation, on bureaucracies and 'babus', who themselves represent a force of the status quo.

Beyond this organisational and institutional incapability it is the politics, prejudice, mistrust and territorial issues among states that keep things gridlocked.

Yet there are successful examples of 'bottom up' development initiatives in South Asia which include India's Amul dairy farmers' cooperative model, Pakistan's Orangi Pilot Project and Bangladesh's Grameen Bank and these ought to be replicated across South Asia.

The coming decades cannot afford to be squandered. The consequence of that would be catastrophic and would condemn too much of humanity to permanent backwardness and misery.

RETHINKING CITIES

November 2014

FROM antiquity, cities have performed political and commercial functions and served as cultural and social centres. In recent history, the ideas of the Renaissance were incubated in Florence. From here they grew out and ignited the Industrial Revolution which paved the way for the rise of Western civilisation. Cities were small and compact.

Ours too were dense cities, with skill and professional clusters and culture. Go back to pre-colonial Peshawar. Inside the walled city you would find clusters of dentists, potters, money changers and coppersmiths. In Qissa Khwani bazaar, listen! Story poems (badalas) recited beautifully to interested, inquiring audiences in dense urban, commercial settings.

But now we have uncultured suburban sprawl where once was a vibrant city. Why?

The car and cheap oil changed the anatomy of cities everywhere. In addition, bureaucratic and pretentious planning believed life could be segmented into compartments of commerce, housing and entertainment. The result was complex zoning laws that spread the city far and wide, making people hostage to cars. Wide avenues, underpasses and overhead highways became the arteries of cities while people were hived into housing colonies to work in distant commercial areas and seek officialdom in still distant compartments.

Not surprisingly, community, culture, public space and life were crowded out. The cosmopolitan city experience that energised Leonardo, Dickens, Picasso, Marquez and Iqbal has been strangled by the car and that new priesthood, the urban planner. As a result, density has given gave way to sprawl; community to heightened individualism; and sidewalk, walkability and human interaction to the automobile.

The post-colonial bureaucracy who had gained control of our cities' inherited elite, publicly owned housing for private use. It didn't take it long to realise that zoning could be a lucrative rent-seeking game and land development could bring personal rewards.

The result was sprawling DHAs and similar developments for the rich, in some places eating up valuable agricultural land — 200 years of irrigation investments — which continue to be converted into suburban housing year after year. Karachi's protected mangrove forests could face similar predation. Of course, the poor were zoned out of the system and thrown to squatter settlements to suffer epithets of 'informal' and 'illegal'.

So if cites are engines of growth, are we giving ours traction to pull the economy? Karachi has grown rapidly into an unmanageable urban mess. What can we learn from experience elsewhere?

Bogotá was a troubled city, characterised by drugs, conflict, lawlessness and crime. It was without self-esteem and ownership, its quality of life one of the lowest in Latin America. Yet a city governance model transformed Bogotá in the course of a decade. Copying isolated projects of Bogotá, (like the Metro buses) does not bring transformation without including the kernel ingredients of the policy: densification, high rise — mixed use developments, walkability and improved citizenship.

The current paradigm favouring cars and sprawl must change to one that favours people, community and life. Bogotá's dangerous ghettos and slums have been opened up by a wide strip of 27 kilometres featuring play spaces, park land and walking and cycling tracks. Such initiatives nurture identity, encourage volunteerism, and have been known to improve citizenship and reduce crime rates.

Cities and citizens thrive when culture thrives. In contrast we have seen cultural focal points including foreign ones such as the Goethe Institutes and Alliance Française centres in our cities diminish. Cultural vitalisation begins with 'place-making' — creating destinations that people want to go to. Streets, public markets, waterfronts, public buildings, libraries, exhibition centres, museums, downtowns, squares and parks are foundations of civil society and cornerstones of democracy. Culturally vibrant cities are creative cities. They catalyse innovation, private investment and foster grass-roots entrepreneurial activities.

Transformation, how? By writing new rules to change rules.Developing new zoning regulations to favour high density, mixed use developments over sprawl, favouring public transport over cars and creating public spaces for cultural revitalisation.

The maze of bureaucracies and antiquated regulations only perpetuate status quo and foster entropy. They need to be replaced with autonomous city governments that can reduce over-regulation, allow urban reform and bring in open, consultative policy and decision-making mechanisms. With its road map to achieve transformation, Bogotá was able to increase city revenues. It was able to bring in private investment through public-private partnership mechanisms and float municipal bonds to raise money for transformation.

The genius of turning our cities to become engines of growth already exists in our people. All they need is to be given an enabling environment.

Co-authored with Nadeem ul Haq, former Deputy Chairman, Planning Commission of Pakistan

IRON ORE 'DISCOVERY'

February 2015

ON that bright sunny morning, the villagers must have been delighted at the unusual sight of a small propeller plane flying over their fields. It was the 1970s, and the OGDC's aircraft was conducting an aeromagnetic survey over northern Punjab.

As it repeatedly flew over in a grid-like pattern, it was detecting a magnetic anomaly near Chiniot, pointing to the possible presence of iron ore beneath the surface. The aircraft returned to base, the data was logged and the matter rested.

It wasn't until 1989 that the Geological Survey of Pakistan picked up the dusty file and carried out a geophysical survey, in which a small ore body was identified. Nevertheless, a geophysical survey is a limited study and does not confirm the resource with the degree of certitude that would motivate commercial interest. That would require more detailed investigations.

Yet another decade passed when in 1999, the Punjab Mineral Development Company commissioned an international geological firm to carry out the detailed investigations over a small 'area. After digging boreholes it confirmed the presence of a small deposit of iron ore.

While the size of the deposit was of little commercial value, more importantly, the investigations, using extrapolations and inferences from the collected data, pointed to the presence of much greater quantities of iron ore (in addition to other minerals) — over 500 million tons — in the wider area. However, to confirm that would require a larger, detailed investigation. At that the matter rested.

In 2009 I had accepted a position with the Punjab Board of Investment and Trade. It was apparent to me that Chief Minister Shahbaz Sharif understood the subject of iron and steel well. Perhaps for that reason I picked up this initiative as my pet project.

In November 2009 I commenced a series of strategic conversations across a range of stakeholders, businessmen and technical experts in the field who were conversant with the subject. What do we do with these bits and fragments of geological information? What would it take to have this classified as a proven reserve? And afterwards who would invest in this mega mining project?

What would be the terms of the transaction? What kind of mining methodology would be required? What kind of logistic and transport infrastructure would be needed to remove earth to the depth of a 30-storey building and then haul the millions of tons of excavated ore?

How would we depopulate the hundreds of acres of farmland and villages — underneath which the ore was located? What would we do with the iron ore? Could we convert some of it to steel? If so, where would the energy come from in an already energy-starved country? Could we also sell some of the raw iron ore?

By April 2010 our rigorous consultations had led to the development of a road map that staked out a path to commercially tap these resources. The first requirement was to carry out a full-blown geological investigation that would authenticate these deposits to an acceptable international standard. And even with the chief minister applying full force, it took a slothful Punjab bureaucracy nearly half a decade to get this done.

But finally it has happened. A Chinese company has authenticated the deposit to be qualified as "reserves". And while they are sizeable they are not very large by global standards. The entire reserve quantity is little more than what Australian mining giant BHP-Billiton would typically produce in two years.

The hard work only now begins. The ore is lodged deep under the surface. The area is well drained by the Chenab river, which may pose hydraulic challenges during excavation. The resulting mining solution could be costly.

That would make the Punjab iron ore project marginal on a world scale. Any investor will look at a range of comparable mines in the world's ore-producing regions and compare the extraction costs per ton. And in the presently oversupplied world market many marginal mines have become dormant and are available.

Then getting the land cleared would pose a challenge for the Punjab government. The land acquisition for the Mangla reservoir expansion took years.

Structuring a mining concession, especially against the backdrop of the Reko Diq fiasco, will pose another challenge.

If the project envisages steel production on site then the government will have to think about ways to provide energy — either coking coal or gas.

Finally, to move ore (and even steel) through overland transport to our steel mills and ports requires a modern, heavy haul rail system.

We will turn to ways of addressing these challenges at a later time.

MOTORWAYS NEEDED?

March 2015

O N a recent visit to Karachi the prime minister announced plans to build a Karachi-Lahore motorway. The groundbreaking of the first segment from Karachi to Hyderabad was also performed. The existing four lane Karachi-Hyderabad 'super highway' is in rundown condition. The plan is to upgrade it to a six-lane motorway, fenced on both sides.

This is to be done in public-private-partnership, a mode known as rehabilitate-operate-transfer. Under this, a private investor would upgrade the road at his own cost and then operate it for 25 years during which the investment would be recovered, the main revenue coming from toll collection. In this way, the government says the project would not require public funds.

This is all very well on paper; except when we examine the track record, successive governments have tried and been unable to make this scheme work. A 'groundbreaking' of this nature has been done before. One fails to see what will be done now that is characteristically different from previous attempts. I will return in a moment to why these past attempts didn't work. But first let's look at where we are going with our national development priorities.

In Pakistan, the main instrument for financing development is the Public Sector Development Programme (PSDP) of the federal budget. This includes heads for infrastructure and social sector components. Pakistan has grossly neglected its social sector (read human development) responsibilities and this has led to the present problems of unchecked population growth, appalling levels of education enrolment, skills development and healthcare provision, leading to rampant poverty, unemployment and lawlessness.

On the infrastructure side, Pakistan spends little over 2pc of GDP on capital spending on physical infrastructure. This is the lowest among peer countries. A 2011 working paper titled Public Investment Program Phase-I Report on Macro-Fiscal and Development Framework by Hafiz Pasha et al (among them Saqib Sherani) observed that Pakistan remained over-invested in roads; meanwhile railways, ports and the water sector remained insufficiently funded.

With the 18th Amendment, most of the PSDP subjects and funds have been transferred to the provinces and it is hoped that the provinces will now pay more attention to the human development factor. With the remaining federal funds the priority areas would appear to be building water storage, improving watercourses and restructuring the railways.

Which brings us to the question, do we need more motorways? Regional connectivity and the Pak-China corridor are important but why can't these be built, for the most part, on the back of upgrading existing highways, building fuel pipelines and restructuring the rail system?

To date I have not seen a study on the socio-economic benefits that have accrued from building the Lahore-Islamabad motorway. Have the original objectives laid down in 1993 been met? And how do these benefits compare with alternative project opportunities that may have been available at that time? It is also worth observing that simple things like the new traffic policing systems introduced in Lahore and Islamabad in recent years have in fact brought greater everyday life and economic benefits to the citizens of these cities than the motorway.

According to the Pasha-Sherani report: to 'crowd in' sustained private investment requires more than just a high level of public investment in physical infrastructure and development of human capital. It requires the government to play its role as an 'enabler' (or facilitator) in the economy, by providing the appropriate institutional framework, including laws and regulations, such as guaranteeing property rights, providing for contract enforcement and dispute resolution mechanisms.

In this way, the tough laws on cheque bouncing for instance, may have had a more palpable effect on the economy (by building trust in economic transactions) than the building of expensive flyovers.

And that also explains why previous attempts at upgrading the Karachi-Hyderabad 'super highway' under the public-private-partnership mode have failed. Why Reko Diq turned into a fiasco. And why Pakistan Steel and the Railways continue to languish.

Recently Finance Minister Dar has spoken of the need for a 'Charter of Economy', a minimum economic agenda that may be agreed by all political parties to repair Pakistan's serious economic dysfunction. One of the bullet point items on that agenda ought to be the determination of national development priorities governing the use of PSDP funds. While the provinces can focus on human development, the guiding principles for the centre should be to focus on schemes that will kick-start growth, bring about equitable distribution, improve productivity, create a high multiplier effect, and crowd in private investment. If we look around, are the motorways the best schemes available to do that? Or can we identify others?

TUMULT ON THE
KARACHI STOCK EXCHANGE

April 2015

THE story begins in January 2015 when a little known Miami-based fund, Everest Capital suffered crippling losses in currency trading. CNBC reported that a single bad bet on the Swiss franc may have caused $860 million of its total $3 billion assets under management being wiped out.

It was fast becoming apparent to the financial community that the fund's investors would soon be lining up outside its doors to redeem their investments and salvage what remained of them.

According to a Bloomberg news article, a significant portion of Everest's investments were parked in emerging and frontier markets and across different asset classes. These included a real estate company in the United Arab Emirates, minority equity positions in some Indian banks, Chinese internet companies, Brazilian education firms and banks as well as renewable energy projects across emerging markets — in investor parlance known as FDI (foreign direct investment). In Pakistan, Everest's investments were in equities — termed as FPI (foreign portfolio investment) — that brokers at the Karachi Stock Exchange estimated at $150m.

Stock market investments (FPI) are relatively easier to liquidate — and therefore more volatile — than FDI. That when the crunch came, Everest would aggressively sell off its portfolio investment in Pakistan, was a foregone conclusion for those who knew the goings on in January 2015.

Yet, Everest's $150m portfolio constituted only a tiny part of the total nearly $6.6bn (around 2pc) of FPI in Pakistan. This meant it should not have caused a major disruption on the bourse. Yet it did. Here's what happened:

By late January, sizeable foreign selling became discernible on the Karachi Stock Exchange. Everest had clearly begun to offload its Pakistan portfolio. But something else was also at work. A Feb 5 report in the local English press mentioned that on Feb 3 "out of nowhere, the sponsors of K-

Electric have offloaded 4pc of their stake on the Karachi Stock Exchange". The next day the KSE100 index decline began. Interestingly, Abraaj operates in roughly similar markets and asset classes as does Everest.

In its morning call of Feb 13 2015, circulated to its clients, leading stockbroker JS Investments highlighted that during the previous 15 trading sessions $65.6m in FPI had been pulled out, causing the index to sharply decline as fears of further selling from the foreign front crept in. Of this "around $53m net selling was witnessed in the electricity sector where Abraaj offloaded shares worth $65m in K-Electric," the report said.

This was a major sell-off in a market that was already bracing for decline. As prices fell, Everest Capital intensified its distress sale and by March 13, the KSE100 was down 6.5pc from its peak at the start of February. But even more ominous to investors was the flow of steady data indicating sustained foreign selling. The figures included the total of $65m by Abraaj and whatever proportion of its $150m that Everest had sold.

All it takes at moments like this is for somebody to shout 'fire'! And a stampede to the exit door follows. By March 30 the index had tumbled nearly 15pc which meant that over $10bn in investors' assets had been wiped out. Those who rushed to the exit door were mainly leveraged investors; capital protected funds that guarantee the principal amount will not be lost. Interestingly none of the other foreign funds chose to exit despite rumours to the effect.

Then of course the expected thing happened. Markets emerge stronger after such shakeouts. The index went on rebound as investors flocked to pick up stocks at mouthwatering prices. Measured on forward earnings, Pakistani equities still trade at less than 50pc of those in peer economies (India, Indonesia, Philippines and Thailand) and as such will remain attractive for a long time.

The panic was entirely unjustified. Political risk and macroeconomic fundamentals have not been better in a long time. Low oil prices have brought down inflation and government deficits. Interest rates have been lowered. LNG and renewable energy have begun to arrive in the system. Moody's has upgraded Pakistan's bond rating and remittances continue to rise. Pakistan has successfully completed an International Monetary Fund programme and is qualified for further funding. And on the political front an anti-terrorism strategy is being implemented and there has not been much blowback.

Meanwhile, Pakistan awaits the arrival of the Chinese president this week during which major agreements are likely to be signed on the Pak-China corridor. With its new Asian Infrastructure Investment Bank, China also appears to now have a mechanism to finance these projects. Further down the horizon lie the government's privatisation and power-sector reform agendas.

After the tumult, there may be a fair bit of good news for KSE investors in the days to come.

A MASS TRANSIT SYSTEM FOR KARACHI

June 2015

WHEN the Punjab government was building its metro bus, what was Sindh doing? Between 2010 and 2012, the Sindh government, with Japanese assistance drew up a transport master plan for Karachi which envisaged six bus rapid transit (BRT) corridors, two light rail mass transit corridors and revival of the Karachi Circular Railway (KCR).

To get an update on progress I spent an afternoon with Tuaha Farooqui, secretary to the government of Sindh, transport & mass transit department in his office. I felt I should share some of the details with my readers.

I was informed that the feasibility and detailed corridor designs for five BRT corridors have been completed. What was encouraging was that the Sindh government was planning to implement the system in a manner that would involve minimum public funds from the provincial kitty.

The Yellow line concession had just been awarded to a Chinese firm that was shortly going to start construction under the build-operate-transfer (BOT) mode. This is unlike Lahore and Islamabad where BRT projects were built with public funds.

Meanwhile, the Red line had been designed with assistance from the Asian Development Bank (ADB) that had also prepared the integration plan for all lines. The Sindh government would put up only 15pc of the funds for the Red line, the secretary explained, while 85pc would be arranged from the Eximbank of the supplier country. This is quite plausible since from my understanding ADB would have prepared the project documents to a highly bankable standard.

For the Green line, the federal government had agreed to finance the development of infrastructure. The release of funds was in an advanced stage of approval and once disbursed, work would begin. My own conjecture is that during construction the Sindh government would have time to tender out the project to a private concessionaire who would finance the buses and operate the corridor.

For the Blue line, Bahria Town had offered an unsolicited proposal to undertake the complete project in BOT mode. The Sindh government now needs to process this proposal under its public-private partnership framework so that construction can start.

The Orange line is the only one that is funded entirely from public funds and for which the allocation has been made in the present Sindh budget and the PC-1 is being prepared by the National Engineering Services Pakistan.

It is interesting that the Karachi BRT corridors, as planned, are substantially cheaper on a per kilometre basis compared to Lahore and Islamabad (the secretary showed me documents whereby the engineering, procurement & construction cost of Karachi's Yellow line was Rs653 million per kilometre while for Lahore it was over Rs1.1 billion). Even that, for the most part, is being funded by the investor under BOT mode.

It appears Sindh is planning to get all five lines for less money than it cost to finance the Islamabad metro bus corridor. This way the Sindh development budget can be used to meet other urgent needs.

Reviving the KCR, while important, is a relatively long gestation project, considering an investor has not yet been found, even if the plan is ready for execution. But it appeared to me that the five bus corridors are doable before elections in 2018. And though it is a real opportunity, the big question is; can the Sindh government in its present doldrums make this happen?

One good thing is that the government component of funds has already been allocated. So what needs to happen now for the Sindh government to be cutting ribbons before end of 2017?

First off, the Sindh Mass Transit Authority needs to be immediately constituted. The delay in passing the required legislation is not understandable. The Asian Development Bank has also agreed to assist in building and strengthening the authority once it comes into existence. Secondly, it appears to me that a strong and credible political person should take ownership and become the moving force behind (and the face of) the initiative. Usually that would be the mayor. But within Sindh's ruling party is there a possible candidate?

Working under that person, the new authority can expedite the processes so work starts early on all corridors. They will need to ensure no show stoppers are allowed to stall work — such as resistance from vested interests, ambiguity and disputes over contractual terms, and things such as relocation of power lines, poles or transformers.

Construction work on these multiple projects will also cause a traffic upheaval on Karachi's major arteries for months — M.A Jinnah Road, Sharea Faisal, Rashid Minhas Road, Korangi Road, Shahrah-i-Quaideen and University Road. Everything needs to be foreseen and dealt with before work begins.

It is an arduous task but may be a last opportunity for Sindh's ruling party to redeem itself in the eyes of Karachi's citizens.

IMPROVED TRANSPORT

November 2015

I HAVE to admit that I was a reluctant and late convert to the idea of the Lahore Orange Line metro train project. For those readers less familiar with Lahore, this 27-kilometre path represents a northern arc that skirts the older half of Lahore, stretching from Sher Shah Suri's GT Road, where it enters Pakistan, then travelling through some of the most congested urban real estate in the country before emerging right on the other side, just beyond Thokar Niaz Beg near the M2 motorway. Before anything else, a word of praise is due here for the Punjab government in clearing the path in record time.

Let me sidestep the concern raised about the project being hazardous to heritage sites. I will return to that in a moment. I want to pick up a concern that the Planning Commission had raised but then we hear no more of it: how will the project sustain itself financially? Now whether or not the Planning Commission has a say in a provincial matter, the Punjab government does need to explain that to the public. Pending that, here's some numbers.

A Chinese consortium which includes China Rail and Norinco has contracted to build an elevated and underground rail line. Subsequently, it will bring in the trains and accessories under a procurement contract. All the civil works and equipment would become property of the Punjab government. Against this a loan facility of $1.6 billion would be created and this amount, together with an expected 2pc interest would be paid back by the Punjab government over 20 years to the Chinese EXIM Bank.

Besides loan repayment, the project would also incur annual and recurring maintenance costs, on items not covered under warranty and these would be borne by the Punjab government. Finally, as is usual in arrangements of this nature, the operator (in this case the Chinese consortium) will receive a management fee for operating the scheme as per prescribed schedule, performing maintenance works and adhering to the service-level agreements which form a part of the operating contract.

According to my back-of-the-envelope calculations and pending those numbers from the Punjab government, it will be liable for upwards of $300,000 per day (most of this amount is loan repayment) — every day for 20 years.

Now let's turn to revenue and don't worry if you don't follow the number crunching. Just bear with the flow. The Orange Line has a planned capacity of 250,000 passengers per day. Lahorites undertake an estimated 10 million trips per day and half of those are on public transport. Most of the remaining are on motorcycles. It is therefore not hard to conceive that the Orange Line could be running to capacity in a couple of years.

Now, to break-even at that capacity, the fare would need to be priced at Rs130. Considering the metro bus fare is Rs40 and it carries nearly 200,000 commuters each day, the Punjab government could conceivably price the Orange Line fare at Rs65 which would be half that needed to achieve break-even. That would leave a deficit of $150,000 per day or approximately Rs6bn per year. Is that material? I do not think so. Especially given that most of that could probably be recovered by real estate and advertising revenues that mass transit schemes can generate.

And even if a small deficit shows up every year, the argument is that the public goods that efficient mass transit schemes produce are worth far more. These include reduction in congestion, more dignified transport and productivity gains for citizens, a cleaner more pleasing urban environment and the list can go on.

Having said that, the Punjab government must fully address and satisfy the concerns on hazards to heritage sites like Chauburji and Shalamar gardens which have been raised by Unesco and the Lahore civil society. It must also address the Planning Commission's concern on the process by which the contractor was selected.

I am also aware that the Sindh government is preparing to implement a big bang mass transit scheme for Karachi which envisages five bus rapid transit (BRT) lines and it would be best were that information to be put out on a website so citizens can become engaged early. For most of our history, a centralised federal structure controlled by bureaucrats from Islamabad held back the development of our cities.

The 18th Amendment and NFC award have transferred powers and funds to the provinces and unclogged the system. In the next logical step I hope to see strong city governments emerge and take the reins to turn our cities into the engines of growth that they need to become.

WHAT'S COMING

August 2015

WHAT does the near future hold for Pakistan? How will our lives improve, and on what fronts in the next three or four years? Pakistanis may have a few things to look forward to.

The security operations led by Zarb-i-Azb have already started contributing to a safer national environment and there has not been a blowback on the scale earlier feared. Meanwhile, it appears Punjab is also gearing up to take on the core of urban-based religious extremism. This year saw Independence Day being celebrated with record patriotic fervor. And even if the luxury hotels still continue to resemble bunkers under siege, all indications are that more people will spend more time outdoors.

As a result one can expect to see more family participation at outdoor events and safer public spaces such as town squares, parks, promenades, food streets, exhibitions and 'pedestrianised' walkways. All of these would in turn be made more accessible by growing public transport. This is a congenial setting for the revival of cultural activity, something that has been missing from our milieu for a long time.

I mentioned public transport because with BRT (bus rapid transit) systems being rolled out across major cities, we can expect thousands of people to move in traffic-high density corridors every hour. Empirically, public transport schemes such as this have made for safer cities in other developing countries.

With Lahore and Islamabad already under way, five new corridors are planned for Karachi of which groundwork on three is set to begin. Peshawar and Multan will also see similar schemes in the near future. With that, we can expect to see a reduction in motorcycle traffic and clearer roads in our major cities. As it evolves, rapid mass transit will also have a bearing on the cities' potential to sprawl out further and thereby reduce congestion and temper property prices. Pakistani cities are small and compact by world standards. They don't necessarily have to stay that way.

Sindh has nearly completed the process of digitising its land record. Punjab and Khyber Pakhtunkhwa are not far behind. My friend Zulfiqar Ali Shah, member, Board of Revenue Sindh tells me that "security of land titles will hugely reduce land grabbing and corruption, it will reduce conflict in society and once the services are launched for the public, it will create a massive and fluid market for land transactions. It will greatly ease the process for property to be collateralised for bank loans". His database includes records of 10 million acres of rural and urban land belonging to four million owners of residential, commercial and agricultural property in Sindh. My banker friends confirm that once unleashed, this could spur a boom in mortgage and small business financing as well as agriculture loans. One loses count of the number of positive benefits that will accrue to the citizens in the years to come.

Over the last year, Pakistanis have enjoyed a strong rupee, low inflation and the lowest interest rate in decades. Most of that can be attributed to the sharp fall in oil prices. The flow of funds from the IMF and the successful offer of an international Sukuk have also augmented foreign currency reserves. By all indications the Pak rupee would retain its strength while most other currencies, including the Chinese yuan appear to be losing value.

This could be a boon to a consumer economy, automobiles, electronics and food franchises while keeping inflation in check. Meanwhile, the stock market is expected to maintain its bullish trend amidst rising reserves, improving security environment and infrastructure development activity spurred by the China Pakistan Economic Corridor.

On the energy front, the Punjab-based distribution companies are likely to be privatised and losses and leakages plugged. Consumers may thereby experience some let-up in the power outages. They can also expect further relief on power tariffs and petrol prices because of sustained low oil prices, especially once Iran ramps up oil production after sanctions are removed.

Early next year Pakistan's democratic project enters its ninth consecutive year. By this time there would be functioning elected local governments in place. Not only would democracy have deepened but with that, one could expect more functional and accountable delivery of local and municipal services.

While it is true that a lot more needs to be done on building credible policing, healthcare and education systems, it appears that for most Pakistanis, the coming three to four years would be better than the previous three to four years. We can even expect international cricket to return to Pakistan. And while most of this improvement can be attributed to the fall in oil prices and the security operations, some of it may be the early fruits of the democratic project. And that show must go on.